T0368285

DIVINE SPIRITS *Speak*

A Guide for the Bended Ear

KAREN NJERI KING

AuthorHouse™
1663 Liberty Drive
Bloomington, IN 47403
www.authorhouse.com
Phone: 1 (800) 839-8640

© 2019 Karen Njeri King. All rights reserved.

No part of this book may be reproduced, stored in a retrieval system,
or transmitted by any means without the written permission of the author.

Published by AuthorHouse 01/12/2019

ISBN: 978-1-5462-7216-8 (sc)
ISBN: 978-1-5462-7215-1 (e)

Library of Congress Control Number: 2018914229

Print information available on the last page.

Any people depicted in stock imagery provided by Getty Images are models,
and such images are being used for illustrative purposes only.
Certain stock imagery © Getty Images.

This book is printed on acid-free paper.

Because of the dynamic nature of the Internet, any web addresses or links contained in this book may have changed
since publication and may no longer be valid. The views expressed in this work are solely those of the author and do not
necessarily reflect the views of the publisher, and the publisher hereby disclaims any responsibility for them.

authorHOUSE®

Divine Spirits Speak is for all who seek guidance; however, spiritual guidance is not easy.

Divine Spirits Speak will have you coming back for more because it is one of a kind.

You have to believe and have faith in yourself to understand truths.

Be ready to set your spirit free and rise up from your daily burdens.

Divine Spirits Speak is for you.

Soar to new heights and live an introspective life from those who seek to see you soar.

The reader must be open and ready to hear the words, for there is no other.

CONTENTS

Preface 1

With Profound Gratitude 3

I would like to thank 5

The Spring Solstice 6

Love Is 7

Love Is 8

Love 9

Looking for Love 10

Love 12

Sincerity 13

Friendship 14

Marriage 16

Marriage Is 17

A Mother's Love 18

Birth 19

Rearing of Children 20

Judging—Youthful Folly 22

Fly Free 27

Freedom 28

Manhood Training 29

The Family Unit 31

Transitions 32

Guidance 36

Deception 37

Integrity 38

Progress 40

Faith 41

Gratitude..42

Gratitude..44

Happiness...47

Discipline...48

Patience...53

How to Cultivate Patience, a Virtue....................................59

Oceans of Patience...61

Sitting Still..63

Unselfishness...65

Change...67

Gradual Progress..69

Spiritual Departure..70

Detachments..72

Letting Go..73

Limitations...77

Sensitivity..79

Marathon Runner...80

Opposites...81

Elders...84

Our Creations..85

Butterfly...87

Landscaping...89

Kente..91

Jewels...93

Writings...94

Consultation..95

Fear..97

Decisions..98

Spiritual Life..99

Jealous Spirits...100

Warrior Spirits..101

Spirit...102

How to Cultivate Spiritual Strength 104
Spiritual Growth 105
The Present 106
Stillness 108
About the Scribe 112

PREFACE

Divine Spirits Speak: A Guide for the Bended Ear is written to give direction to the lives of those who seek order about developing themselves in their lifetime. You can begin anywhere you choose because every lesson in this book will be worth learning and incorporating into your goals for success. Attempts to change your life will only meet with triumphs, which will lead you on a path of an enhanced understanding of this road called life. You will be guided on: raising children, friendship, love, marriage, transitioning or passing on, patience, trust, gratitude, and much more. You will want to share what you will read because it is for all spirits.

Live your life through new eyes and thoughts. Your life can have abundant blessings because you will be more receptive to gratitude and have a greater insight to turn a small step into a qualitative and quantitative leap. This book is for those who will dare to take the journey on the road to a more developed spiritual life. Those who have a bended ear are those who are willing to listen and make a change. Situations will arise in life, and everyone always needs to hear sound advice and be encouraged, so these topics are written for you.

Read *Divine Spirits Speak: A Guide for the Bended Ear,* and you will obtain wisdom that can give you the capacity to soar in life. It is the foundation for developing oneself through introspection, which can lead to self-development. You may choose to journal your experiences, which is a method to help you by recording your insights. You may use this book as a guide for helping your children develop strong spiritual lives.

This book is not written to perfect your life. This is a guide that will assist you in living life to the best of your ability. Everyone's level of development is personal and specific. It is not written to measure anyone. Instead, it is written specifically for your enlightenment and to share with anyone whom you may love or respect. Anyone whom you feel has a bended ear and desires to listen to words that will assist that person in growing spiritually can benefit. Having a bended ear can be defined as a person who listens attentively to messages that can change his or her life and help that person have a better understanding of the lessons in life. In order to make changes, listening is critical—thus, the bended ear.

These writings were messages from the Divine Ones and my highly elevated ancestral spirits for many years. There aren't any personal opinions in this book. Each word was written according to what was heard in my time of meditation. It was written as a spiritual guide to live life. It takes time, commitment, trust, and faith to make attempts to work on your spirit and work through obstacles in life. Accept your challenges. These are divine teachings for any of you who has a bended ear.

I have met many people from different denominations and various spiritual traditions. The Akan tradition appealed to my spirit. I read books, received training in the tradition, and visited Ghana. I respect whatever system works for an individual. This work—spiritual work—involves introspection.

Awareness is different than influence. This book was published to create an awareness about how one can develop spiritually. Because it develops an awareness in living life, you may choose to use the book as a guide to work with groups, to form book clubs, to share among family members and guide your children, to use in rites-of-passage groups, and to guide discussions during the holidays. In addition to the book's use as a tool for individualized growth, couples can choose to read topics as a means of growing together.

WITH PROFOUND GRATITUDE

Like a butterfly,

You have sheltered me in a cocoon with lessons unfolding.

Uncovered, and like a butterfly,

You have removed the layers and coverings of the caterpillar, and

You have changed the crawl-like movement.

You have released this caterpillar into a butterfly

With wings of freedom,

With wings of truth,

With wings of clarity,

With wide, colorful wings.

You have enabled me to fly free,

Free from doubt, questioning, hurt, pain, and spiritual binding.

Medaase for the wings of spiritual freedom,

Wings full of color,

With strength that will soar to spiritual heights.

Medaase for the transformation,

Open as the wings to receptivity,

Open to this life as You have ordained it to be,

Anointed and belonging to the warrior shrines.

Please continue to remain with this butterfly, and steer me always in Your direction.

—Nana Afua Senyani Njeri

I WOULD LIKE TO THANK

God Almighty, the Supreme Being;

Maame Senyani, Nana Densu, and Nana Tigare,

along with all the Mother and Father Shrines;

my highly elevated ancestors;

the priest and priestess who initially trained me,

as well as priests who continue to share the divine teachings of the shrines and information about the Akan tradition; and

my family and friends who have supported my work.

—Nana Afua Senyani Njeri

THE SPRING SOLSTICE

This is the time to sow new seeds—the spring solstice. This is the time to plant new seeds for your spirit and set your spirit goals. Review the past but look to the future. What kind of nurturing does your spirit need? Is it patience? Is it gratitude? Is it giving of yourself or taking care of yourself? Is it a diet change with exercise and foods that will help you to have clear thinking? Know what development your spirit needs. This will call for introspection and honesty. You don't want to fool yourself. Take time. Prepare to landscape your spirit. Sow the seeds and then nurture them for growth.

LOVE IS

Love is being at one with the creators of every existence that was and will be.

Our love flows not like the rivers, but of the ocean.

Our love is higher than the highest peak, for We look down at all Our creations to examine the occurrences of each thing at all times. We are the givers of light and have given you the powerful ball of fire to give you light.

And We give you the moon and its many cycles that people say lure them into love.

All Our creations are works of love—Our natural creations.

We want Our children to be at one.

Love is respect for Our woods.

Our divine spirits live in the trees.

That is why when you enter Our forest, you gaze upon Our trees—the might of their trunks, the very beauty in the formation of their limbs, and the color and dimension of the leaves. Love is in all Our creations in nature. The key is to be still. Admire all Our creations, and you will feel love.

LOVE IS

Love is relentless,

Selfless,

Divine,

Accommodating.

Love is

not persuasive,

not consuming,

not draining,

not debilitating,

enhances life,

gives energy.

LOVE

We do not believe that one should fall into love. That is not exemplary behavior for a higher experience because when you fall, you can be injured physically, spiritually, emotionally, and economically. Those who fall into love tend to fall into divorce. When you experience love, We don't want you to have stumbled or fallen for someone but to be standing upright with clear thoughts.

Never waste your energy on ungrateful souls.

Responsibility is one thing; beyond that is something else.

If you know the spirit or the heart, proceed in the way We would advise.

Laziness and selfishness are qualities We find offensive. It deteriorates one's development of the spirit.

We are repulsed by those who are willing to sit and receive handouts. It may not be their way to give or extend a hand, especially when not asked. Giving unconditionally shows love.

This life should not center around yourself. Love is giving not only of material wealth but of spiritual wealth selflessly.

Do for those who deserve your time and love.

Yes, begin to take time to develop your spirit and your physical being. Take walks of movements—one good exercise you call it.

Love is unconditional.

Love is giving to deserving spirits.

LOOKING FOR LOVE

Our children, don't look in your world for love because you will be disappointed every time. It's a delusion to seek happiness in the midst of chaos. Your joy will be in your growth and the steps you take. Your happiness will be in aligning yourself with the Divine Ones and being receptive to Our teachings. And in so doing, you will not experience disappointment or be surprised about people and their behaviors in your world. Nothing will begin to amaze you about their shortcomings. We are not saying you are removed from the behaviors that you see, but you have worked on most of them in the past.

In this incarnation, you work on carrying Us with you at all times. Your steps will be fewer but firmer. Your words will diminish, but when spoken, they will be significant. Those who cannot embrace the thoughts We give to you are of very little significance in your life. They have roles for you always to see and examine good and evil and their many manifestations in life. It is just the way that water, as small a word as it may be, has magnitude.

Water comprises most of our world. It quenches one's thirst and can drown another. It brings about a harvest to one group and devastating floods to another. We will have you speak on Our behalf, and those who listen and are amenable to Our suggestions will grow. Others will remain stagnant; some will choke on their ideas. Dismiss your thoughts about needing humans because they will cause you to focus on them with a misdirected outlook on correct living. Once you abandon your worldly ideas, you will find a treasure that you kindly want everyone to have.

Your treasure will be happiness and everlasting love from Us, your mother and father shrines who created you. We see your attempts to abandon the falsities of living in your world, and as you reach to Us, We will pull you closer. You will learn to find ultimate comfort with this. Our love is relentless, uncompromising, ever encompassing, consistent, and everlasting.

When you feel alone in your world, read this writing. Ask Us to sit with you and surround you with Our love. And remember there are many of Us who hear you and who will come.

Progress is being made. Stilling yourself is more important for you. It takes more discipline for you to remain still and to sit with Us. It was and always will be the safest choice.

LOVE

You do not waste love on those who do not love you.

Be respectful and carry yourself with ease; be poised yet pointed.

Reality is what reality is.

Burden comes from those who do not respect or love you but only prey on you.

Assistance is for those who mean you well and love you.

Your Divine Ones show you pictures so that you can see both paintings.

This is your reality. We are not saying not to do, but not to waste energy with one more than the other.

Your commitment is to the Divine Ones first and foremost and then your husband or your wife.

SINCERITY

Sincerity can only be judged over time. What may appear one way on a given day may appear quite differently over the course of just a few weeks. Always give it time. Never rush anything. Step slowly and methodically. Long-term challenges give long-term strengths. Spiritual development happens over time because only through time can sincerity become apparent. No one can judge another. Always allow the Divine Ones to show others' hands to you. If there is no sincerity, then love cannot exist. Sincerity is one of Our keys to spiritual success.

FRIENDSHIP

Friends are those who will anticipate a problem for you and think of a solution. They safeguard your spirit. They are truthful and honest no matter how you view it. They have an unconditional love no matter what your choices are. They understand you are entitled to choices because that is how one develops character. A friend is conscious of how you feel and thinks of many ways to advise and comfort you. A friend helps with the best spirit choices because his or her ultimate goal for you is to meet with spiritual success in life. That is what brings comfort and true happiness. Encouragement is displayed in abundance.

A friend is trustworthy, loving, and kind. A friend remains constant and not just for a period in time. The level of commitment is different than from an acquaintance. Keep each one with the proper perspective in mind so disappointments don't arise. Be mindful to also understand your friends' limitations, as they are temporarily in human form. Recognize who they are and show gratitude in many ways. But, most importantly, reciprocate the friendship. Do this in the ways that are needed for them.

Friendship must be balanced. It cannot be one-sided, or it will not be a fair relationship. It is not balanced because one does something so the other rushes to do something else. It is done with ease, not perfection. A friend helps you through life's situations. Be mindful of them because they are rare. Friendships develop into loveships over some time, and this is the primary step to love a husband or a wife. We never sanction an easy-come, easy-go friendship or marriage. In most times, it develops from a spiritual relationship from other incarnations, which is why the understanding is so easy. Friends help with worldly resolutions and help to prepare your spirit. A friend is never a traitor, gossiper, or participant in the demise of anyone, including you. Friendship is to be treasured for lifetimes.

Friends are mindful not to hurt each other and defend each other whenever possible. If someone talks about a friend, it is as though that person is talking about you. A friend relationship can be brother to brother, sister to sister, brother to sister, etc. There are very few of these relationships because you would not have time for yourself to develop and grow. Reflect on friendships. If someone ultimately has a totally different goal spiritually, do you think that that person can be a friend? There are differences between acquaintances and friends. Be clear and act accordingly. We urge you to recognize differences.

Conflict and battle do not serve as a base for friendship. If these exist, then become more introspective and wiser about your choices of friends. Keep oneself open to learn and differentiate relationships. These are never rash decisions; it takes meditative thoughts, introspection, and time. Think about each other's backgrounds and experiences. Don't judge; merely observe to understand. It can be traumatic to lead with your heart. Life should always be guided by your spirit first. This is why meditation is an important influence on your development. You are able to hear a voice other than your own or those who do not mean you well. This practice will safeguard your heart and develop your spirit. Love Us unconditionally and you will learn your lessons with ease and not trauma. Be still so that you can gain an understanding of choosing friends in your world.

MARRIAGE

Marriage truly encompasses a linking of like spirits. When We speak of spirits, We are referring to that which is on path with the Divine Ones. This is the only kind of marriage.

With the giving up of themselves for the Shrines, this means that they will be unselfish because they can put many things before themselves. You will see humility before Us and in working with others. Patience will be seen through looking and waiting to see the prior qualities. Can he or she handle pressures? Because when things are rough, do they try to escape or do they face adversities and devise meaningful ways of handling situations.

MARRIAGE IS

The union of spirits is a union of ancestral mothers and fathers, bringing together previous incarnations

Giving relentlessly

Loving unconditionally

Having patience

Showing gratitude

Uttering truths

Building character

Being amenable to suggestions

Sharing

Trusting and being trustworthy

Growing and allowing others to grow at their own pace

Seeking advice from those who are capable

Laughing

Creating companionship

Interdependence and listening

All endured only through the blessings of God

A Mother's Love

A mother's love is all encompassing

It reaches below the sea and raises you up to the sky

Carrying you safely on the back to the end of their time

They stay with you in their time and your time

Being forever protective and watchful

Allowing no one or nothing to take them away from what Divine Ones have produced for them

There aren't enough words to describe a mother's love, but know that her love is protective, relentless, supportive, and bound in the wrappings of the spirit that demonstrates an unconditional love.

Never take it for granted and preserve it in a way that will last you your physical lifetime and your spirit time which is everlasting

A mother's love is everlasting

Speak to her for always

Your Divine Mothers bless you with a worldly mother to set you on a path to know Us, serve Us, respect Us, and love Us

Who could know a Mother's Love but the Mother of Creation. She, your Mother Senyani, is always with you and sending her daughter to protect you because She has taught them well.

BIRTH

Awaiting the birth of a child is your first test in patience as a parent.

The Divine Ones create a process that beholds an inseparable bond between child and parent.

Breathe deeply and allow the child's spirit to come into this world. Ask your highly benevolent ancestors to help with this process as the time passes.

Welcome the spirit of the newborn.

This is the process of bringing spirit life into this world—labors of love, patience, and understanding.

The love for your child supersedes time.

Breath is of the essence for new spirit life to begin.

Rearing of Children

The rearing of children is the ultimate responsibility in spiritual development. One can never imagine the responsibility attached when producing another spirit: spirit child. We say *spirit child* so you know that you are having an impact on the spirit primarily and the child secondarily.

Therefore, when producing a child, it is important that the father and mother are working with divine forces to bless their child in order to help create a healthy child and for the Almighty to bless this union of two spirits. You become responsible to raise a child so that the spirit can grow. If either parent does not understand spiritual development, how can they teach it to their child or children? This is why in your world, unless a child has an impeccable background from previous incarnations of development, that child will grow like a weed and have little or no positive impact in Our world.

Thus, you have the birth of children from addiction or battered children, and We can go on. Everyone as a parent must do his or her best to instill values to nurture the spirit of the child. Those who don't will not meet their ultimate responsibility in life. Teach the spirit about integrity, patience, truth, and love, and you will reap what you sow. As an elder, you will be cared for and not sent away to perish alone. People attach money to the ultimate responsibility; however, it is not the only duty, and it definitely does not come first.

It is the quality of your time and the love expressed that will develop the child into a good parent. People need examples, and effort must be exerted. When you produce a spirit child, you must become selfless to provide the child with his or her needs. How will your spirit child learn to love when he or she has not been loved? When you create spirit children, it is your responsibility to develop these little ones into blessed souls.

Their receptivity is not your responsibility. Your responsibility is to deliver the message of many teachings or lessons so that they have been made aware. Then they make their own choices. This is why you can see that you cannot scatter these seeds around a world and leave them unkept. These actions will weigh heavily against you at your time of judgment. We urge you to understand.

Judging—Youthful Folly

You have asked that We give you the words to answer someone's questions. Tell that person one very important teaching of God, and that is that human beings were created by God and no human being can prejudge another's belief in that which is divine.

He is an infant of God in this work and has no idea yet as to the workings of divine systems. Tell Our son that We embrace your thoughts about divine will, but remember that it is your God who created heaven and earth. It is your God who created man and woman. It is your God Who created ways for all to worship.

Just as each family is made of different members, some who go to school to acquire knowledge and bestow knowledge upon others. Just as some family members work devoutly at sharing health information to provide their temples with the best foods so that they have the will and strength to do the work they have been ordained to do is just the way we send messengers to families to keep them abreast of a path that is most worthy to live.

Don't become frustrated with those who have no understanding. Pray for patience and clarity.

As you remember, he belongs to those Who created him, and Our teachings are always that your work is constant, like Our rivers. Your job is to work on yourself.

There is no room to judge others. You can give them information, and if they choose to have closed ears, then allow them to walk by.

Culture is a means to teach the young to listen to the elders, but you see how some children of God will quote scriptures and quote commandments such as "honor thy father and thy mother." However, they cannot follow a simple direction. This is their work to transfer the written word into the actual deed. This is when that negative spirit in his world, Satan, has his laugh.

Of course, We are here to protect you spiritually, but Our world is made up of different challenges. There are people in your world who are ridden by witch spirits, and their job is to harm others in many possible ways.

This is one of their times of the year right now—the day they call Halloween, which is only about witchcraft.

It is best to shut your doors to these experiences. We created commandments, teaching, and laws unto God to be followed.

He will receive glimpses of light just like all of Our children. Just hold the beam steady, and one glance is progress. Just as you said believing in God does not prevent you from playing ball on a field, he read his scripture and saw a light. He could not see the light when you held the beam.

Some people feel that they must impress others by telling others that they are saved. Being saved is living the word of God day by day, hour by hour, minute by minute, and second by second. Our work is to do less talk and more work on oneself.

No one saves anyone else; this is God's work. The work on self is endless. It takes millenniums to accomplish a single step, as you know this to be true. There are old spirits in your world, as well as baby spirits. The blessing is the realization that a baby is a baby is a baby and to listen to the parent for guidance. Well, you have seen this as you have worked for many incarnations with babies with closed ears thinking that they can lead the parents.

Our daughter, when you feel that the mind or spirit is closed, simply walk away. Because you have been blessed to have direct contact with Divine Spirits, you do not have to subject yourself to those with deaf ears. As you know, leave them with Us.

As they live life with the challenges of your world, they will begin to see, and the beam will show brighter and brighter as to what the true teachings of God really are. Our daughter, We thank you for your strong conviction of the divine and your faith in the power of prayer. We will come to you at your greatest moment and answer your prayers just as you have been awakened to be our scribe.

We know how thankful you are for even one line of blessings, and you are truly welcome because We know your spirit and see your determination to be a devout daughter to Us.

We love you. Continue to drop a seed and leave it to Us to nourish the seed because We can only nourish that seed when it is open and receptive to God's will. Humans have no will; they are nothing until We breathe life into their bodies and into their spirits. Then the seed will take on a form.

If not nourished, it will perish on earth and never see the Spirit World—what some term heaven. "Fear not" does not mean to welcome evil spirits in. Don't test oneself or open yourself for these challenges. We will give enough challenges.

Some children have a deaf ear and have to learn lessons firsthand, which can be a lot harder.

Every day restore your strength with Our love and with Our blessings. Your pace is too fast. Slow down and resume the inner work. Everyone will drain you, and when you look for a cup of tea, you had better store enough energy to heat and pour. Your efforts are not seen for what they are. Your gifts that We have provided you are not highly regarded. Until they are, take care of yourself. We have work for you to do. You will always fight evil in subtle ways and continue to be an example even in the worst of situations.

Advice to help the physical being is valuable in order to live a better life. The faculties must be clear in order to function. Wisdom is advice given or bestowed upon by God. He grants the power to heal the sick when he or she uses remedies that God, the Almighty, has created from the earth.

All that is natural before it is tainted by man. Herbs are life forces from God's earth to help preserve mankind to help him not only grow in years but open up the mental faculties to function at a higher level. Cleansing the blood purifies the soul. Cleanse your spirit and your body, and you cleanse your soul. It is work; it is discipline that leads to what is divine.

Thanks for being receptive to the wisdom of God to assist in the cleansing of the physical being, which can only assist in being pure in spirit. Thank you for allowing yourself to follow truth. Although it may not be the popular manner for healing, it is the authentic system for healing.

Let not people judge you, but always follow the words of your God. God leads you where you need to go. Thank you for siding with truth and assisting those who have the desire to be helped. Your work is appreciated. Our daughter, slow down and breathe.

We see your efforts. Your students appreciate you, but more importantly, We appreciate your efforts. Thank you. We are going. You will fast as you meditate.

People in your world have affinities for living their lives a particular way because of past incarnations, spiritual genetics, desire and inclination to make changes, attributes such as giving of oneself, being sincerely grateful for all that they are given, and many other ways in their lifetimes. Too much cannot be handled at one time, so we give the lesson in bits and pieces to make it bearable to handle or even come to an understanding of what patience and giving up of oneself means. Loving with no chains, adopting grateful spirits, and weaving it into everyday living is more than a task; it is the changing of one's spirit, which is the work. It has nothing to do with judging, pointing fingers, or teaching lessons. We, the parents, teach the lessons.

You are seeing a lot and thinking without your mind, but you are attempting to use your spirit and constantly stop to make the higher choice—the spirit choice. What would the mother and father shrines want me to say, to do, to work on? And this is when We celebrate the work on the spirit from within. We know that it is not easy, and that is why We say that you need patience.

It does not come fast, in a hurry, or in a jiffy. It is the simmering pot that has the most flavors. Your grandmother always told you that a watched pot never cooks. You don't keep opening and stirring, but you give it time. This is true for spiritual development too.

This is why Our son needs to hear the word *spirit* constantly to drop the seed, so when he is among his peers, he will know Our teachings and hear Our words. That way he has a spirit of appreciation and knows gratitude well. The job is not as hard for those with spirits that have developed over time. Younger spirits need more time and patience.

Try to have your ceremony today with your children and speak about the principle and what you do to work at living the principles. This is a guide. *Ujima* means collective work and responsibility. What does it mean to work and not be lazy? Children come into this world choosing parents with a spirit history. They have had previous incarnations, and they choose a path of that which is right or that which is wicked. You can see this early in their development.

Some have manners, and some don't care to hear about the correct code of ethics. Some can work toward Us, and some make every effort to turn away. Don't give wicked children much of your time because they are on their own paths and will cause you to be ill. We love you for questioning and not assuming.

FLY FREE

Birds fly free. They are only hindered by mankind, who chooses to shoot or cage them. They soar with ease and flare. They glide as though they will never hit a pebble, graceful as the lake is calm and different as the species of mankind. Never entrap or cage yourself. Always allow yourself to free your spirit so that it can glide amid the pebbles, never hitting a stone.

Soar with your Divine Mothers' words attached to your wings to give you flight. Be steadfast as you land with the strength of your Divine Fathers as they steer your feet.

We give you the beauty and the stamina, the lightness of the spirit as the wings, and the security of the openness of the claws for landing, allowing you to feel secure. When you think of troubles, take your spirit to flight. You know to use your mind well.

Now use your wings to take flight. Study our creations. Watch them in unison as though they are one. Eat lightly. Speak softly. Walk with ease. Think of the flight and the lightness of the bird, and you will unload some of your weights. As you lighten your load, then you will have an easier flight in this incarnation.

Spread your wings and soar, Our daughter. You are welcome as you sit and listen. You will hear of the path that enables you to be with your ancestral spirits. They walk before you and behind you. We love you.

FREEDOM

Freedom is knowing who is in control of your being, your accomplishments, and your recreation. Freedom is holding gratitude in your spirit for the Divine Ones for what choices They have made for you, thankful for the exposure to life's experiences. Freedom is laying your spirit down before the Divine Ones for them to guide you in what you need to do, say, or not say. Freedom is full acceptance of what was given to you and accepting it with love and gratitude. Freedom is defying that which is not good for you even though your human thoughts want you to have it. *It* is the challenge factor. *It* may not be your challenge that We deem necessary for you in this incarnation.

Freedom is spiritual understanding. It allows you to spread your wings and defy gravity because your flight is a spirit flight. Fly high. This is a spiritual freedom. This is true freedom. Enjoy your spiritual flight to freedom. Freedom awaits with melodic tones to accompany your flight. Never allow clouds to deter your flight.

Manhood Training

Manhood training is designed to prepare young boys to become men or young men to become mature and spiritually prepared men. Organizations should prepare men to hold their heads up with pride in order to serve their Creator and become shining stars in the galaxy. There is nowhere in any organization where this pride is to be beaten unmercifully into a spirit. This is not the manner by which men grow into manhood. As a matter of fact, it becomes quite the contrary. Some male organizations can be evil and abusive, and they may even strip young men of their pride and manhood.

There has always been warrior development that was a disciplinary program, but injuries and beatings are not the prerequisite for the development of warriors. It should involve body strengthening, not bodily deterioration; mind strengthening, not mind degradation; and spiritual development, not spiritual bruising or the spiritual attachment to the evil forces and ways. Organizations of this kind must be founded on principles and not built on a foundation with the demeaning of a character or the defacing of a body that was made by the Creator.

Who has a right to take a man through enslaved procedures? Are you developing men, or are you creating servants? The symbols must be upheld to the standard of which the actual Sphinx was made. Men who are to be developed into the best should not be treated the worst. The leader's job is to guide, protect, and inspire and not allow evil to prevail.

Endangering the physical, emotional, and spiritual life of a man is not creating boys to become men. This behavior is what exists in the prison system and breaks the spirits of those who cohabitate behind bars. Are these young men to be prisoners, or should they be developed into warriors? This is how evil works—in darkness. A higher spiritual path is developed in the light, rising above the evils of this world.

Our sons can no longer have their bodies darkened by the wrath and whipped into submissiveness. Their minds cannot be clouded by liars and thieves as examples, and their spirits cannot be entrusted to the hands of witches. This will never be sanctioned by anyone who chooses a higher, evolved spiritual path. Those who continue to uphold this behavior will be held accountable for their actions because the Creator sees all events in your world. He is the Father of all fathers.

THE FAMILY UNIT

What humans choose to create on earth is a structure in complete opposition to what was designed. As you know, Divine Ones come together to discuss and resolve all issues pending. We never argue but always arrive at an agreement. These families in your land come together to cause disruptions in the lives of most, and they do this through the destruction of or division between the heads of the family, which is the link.

The Divine Ones are always united after a discussion. We have universes to keep functioning. It is not an element in Our fabric; otherwise, you, Our children, wouldn't be able to be given sound advice, and We wouldn't have time to protect you. When a statement is made, We are always thinking of the best and the most high in everything until proven otherwise. In your world, the reverse is the norm. It doesn't have to be this way.

Secrets and deceptive concepts disband a family unit. A wife harbors no secrets from her husband, and he harbors neither surprises nor secrets from his wife. They are joined as one and commit to being one when they take vows. Children may try to divert the energies so that they, in their selfish ways, can get what they want, but parents are the elders and should be wise to children's foolish ways.

Witch spirits achieve success when the fabric of the family is destroyed. Watch those who gloat at mishaps, those who are jealous, and those who cannot accept honor. Adults lead the family. Children watch and learn from the adults. No one is to cause dissension in your family unit. If words are uttered, strike them down.

Transitions

Transition carries one across into a spirit life. Preparing for a transition takes lifetimes. It is a skill of letting go of worldly possessions that you don't even possess. It is true realization that everything has been temporary. Your family, homes, jobs, cars, and money are only temporary. Preparation helps you to use and acknowledge these items for a period of time, and then it is time for a change.

Just like clothing can only be worn for a period of time before the color fades and the fabric looks worn. The same is true for your vehicles (your bodies). The pulse begins to fade, and the organs become worn and deteriorate. The refreshing time—the changing time—is the transitional period when you shed old habits, lifestyles, beliefs, and material things for a new awakening of your spirit. Spiritual change is empowering, strengthening, and everlasting.

Accepting transitioning is what you prepare for as opposed to preparing for passing. This becomes too close to border on suicidal issues. This is when you begin to not safeguard your life and dwell on death. What one does is make final preparations to alleviate the stress on the family and state your desires but then live the life that We have given to you. Your spirit will be lighter when you accept when We send for you, but We don't want you to lie in waiting for us to send for you. When you have made your preparations for leaving the physical world, you have accepted that We will remove you at a time when and how We decide. Making the preparations is an indication of acceptance and preparation.

The spirit work continues until the calls are made and We have made decisions. Illnesses are to slow one down so that thoughts are given about the spirit. Transitioning becomes easier to accept as you have seen siblings depart. Their years are not your years. Each day how life is lived is a measure of life after. So you ask, *Well how do I prepare my spirit?* You know this as the choices that you make and acceptance of letting go. Preparing the family and speaking to the children prepares your spirit. Your acceptance of the life that We have given to you prepares you for acceptance of spirit life. So, as you are in your world day by day, accept the life that you have been given and let gratitude surround your spirit, and then your transition will be made smoothly.

You live your life with high spirited choices. Dwell on the life that you are living and do not rush your spirit. Spiritual development is how you or many serve Us on earth. Are you patient, kind, thoughtful, selfless, and independent from relying on what others can do for you? Joy arrives into the spirit when one becomes grateful for what he or she has been given. Gratitude keeps your spirit singing. It opens you up for acceptance of spiritual changes.

Live a life so that you won't have regrets. Live a life of acceptance and gratitude, and then your spirit feels light and not weighed down with worldly concerns. Trust that you are given exactly what We want you to have. Doing all of these things prepares your spirit for a new life of the everlasting. Speak as though they are your last words. Let your thoughts take you to developing your spirit with ease. No rush, no worries—just listen and teach, and your spirit will be prepared. Seclude yourself at times so that others' troubles do not weigh your spirit down. You are beginning to practice separating those who mean you well, those who are contributors to stress, and those who seek ears to clean off their energies. Realizing this helps you to lift weights from your spirit.

Some act as though they want advice. You may want to suggest for them to journal their issues. No person is responsible for anyone else's spirit. Each one is responsible for his or her own spirit. Continue to do your movements even if they change. We are going. Thank you for taking time to receive Our messages. This is an indication that We are foremost in your spirit.

Transitioning doesn't come by chance. You are walking on a path that is ordained and destined by the choices you make. All decisions are important because they are the determining factors for your vital signs. No age is set for making your transition. It varies and is determined by Us. People always question the person's health, age, and life circumstances, but they don't question the most important aspect of one's life, which is the spiritual journey.

Some make reconciliations before they pass. They attempt to correct many wrongdoings during their incarnations, while others choose to make poor choices without making amends for the ills in their lifetimes whether they are long or short. The period for bereavement should not be long because you only lengthen the time of transition for the person in passing. Send prayers to send them on. No one stands to judge the deceased. We measure their spirits by steps of spiritual development from one life to the next.

The spirit to take account for is solely your own. This is the one to work on, to make changes with, to evaluate, and to become introspective on how to develop the changes that are necessary. We send spirits into your world to accomplish tasks, and that can last for the length of time We determine. You may choose a place for the physical body to reside without the spirit. The rest of the choices were made based on your daily efforts to live your life. Everyone has a script for his or her story, which can only be told by that person and only judged by Us, the Divine Ones. Never waste time on speculations. Spend time on acceptance, gratitude, and your individual spiritual work.

GUIDANCE

You are practicing to be in flight when you come to the Spiritual Ones for guidance.

When you close your worldly eyes and open your spirit, We can then communicate with you. Keep this openness, and your wings will be free from soot and debris. This will make your wings lighter and more beautiful. The spirit eye has clear vision and is above your world. This eye does not blink, so it does not see hit and miss.

It is constant. It is consistent. It is accurate because, of course, it is divining. This is the eye that can see into the pot. You can gaze and gaze and gaze, but you are blind if you are not looking on with a spiritual vision.

What We welcome is your heart. This is your centerpiece of your platter. You cannot exist without your heart, so if you offer this to Us, We will know that your love is sincere and your work is internal.

You may be in this world, but you do not have to be of this world. Do not move with emotions; move instead with spiritual backing. You are practicing to be in flight when you come to the Spiritual Ones for guidance. Balance being single. We see your urgency to remain balanced. We see your efforts but be patient.

It takes time for scales to balance when you have just placed the weight on the scale. But after you take the time to set your question on the scale, give it time to settle and sway, and when it stops, you will begin to be able to read it accurately. We are here to strengthen you not weaken you. Perfection is not in your world.

DECEPTION

Deception is the act of the attempt to deceive someone. It is when a person attempts to keep the full information, the full facts, and the thoughts behind a question or discussion from others. A spiritual life reacts to deceitful behavior when it is uncovered or revealed because truth prevails over deceit. It becomes a fine line or a partnership with evil.

What would be a reason to clearly misinform, hide information, and twist the truth? It is always revealed. There is infinite wisdom in stating the facts and revealing information that has no loopholes and no underlying reasons for unclear discussions. We rather the information, the questions, or the discussions be clear and unfiltered from facts and an honest discussion. Never dip your spirit in mud with deceptive conversations because the only one left unclean, unclear, and tainted is the deceptive one.

We train Our children to trust but also to listen to decipher between those who have deceptive ways. It is not meant to alienate them but to be aware of what deception will do because the ultimate truth will be heard and uncovered. Truths are not held under rocks. They bathe in the sun. Deception is not an act or a lifestyle of those who seek higher spiritual living. You have seen this with those who visit with an agenda, saying they desire a visit when no sooner are they in the door than they request a reading—those who ask questions to have you respond to set a stage.

You are not the pawns on this board of life. You always speak truth and can only accept truths. Deception is not truth. Deception manipulates the truth. Choices are to live under a rock or reside with the light of the sun. We never choose darkness over the light. Observe the language of people; listen carefully so that you can ascertain their true ways. Do not be angered; just be aware. It is the spirit that is deceptive. Deceptive spirits remain in darkness. Dark spirits desire to change your temperament and your vision. Our spirits grant you clarity. Clarity doesn't necessarily surface because of age but because of a high, spiritually evolved life. It comes to those who seek answers and rely on the Divine Ones to give the answers, observing and not being judgmental. Life is light. Live in the light.

INTEGRITY

Many people cheat and start ahead in a race. Some may stick a foot out to trip someone else or elbow another in the run or have a conversation to divert someone else's energy or concentration. But integrity is doing things the correct way whether you win or lose at the finish line. When you run with integrity, you're always a winner in the big race—the race of living. There isn't a medal or trophy that gives you such pride. Run the race of integrity, for it outshines the gold, silver, and bronze medals.

It is easy. Well, preparation is of the essence, and the stretching of the spirit exercises consistently when temptation is in the air. Clarity helps you to see the path ahead and the determination to run to the finish line without listening to those negative voices. Others may say to wait and run in the next race, but there's no need for postponement because no matter when the race occurs, all of the elements—effort, consistency, clarity, determination, and integrity—must be included.

Is there a perfect race? *Never.* The muscles always ache from contracting and releasing. Just as the mind tries to make decisions, it contracts and releases. But when the foundation is laid and integrity is upheld, whether the crowd sees you tear the tape or not, the Divine Ones smile upon the job you've done staying in your lane of integrity and following the path of the highest morals and values. For that reason, it's golden. It outshines any other behavior, and it glows.

This is the reason to uphold the integrity of the Divine Ones. Our values and morals are everlasting. We were before rivers ran and the sun shone. There is always a marathon between good and evil. You will always have the cheaters. Know not to do this. You will always have the hecklers attempting to discourage you.

There will be those spirits who trip you and even make you fall. But in the race of life, you should always be aware that hecklers can lose their voices, and those spirits who may trip you will fall themselves because it is always the feet of your Divine Ones that carry you to the finish line.

What better cheering to hear than the strong sounds of a stadium of melodic cheers or the rays of the sun beaming across the field with rainbows at the finish line. You can sign up—put your name on the board. We will always be the wind beneath your wings. Your family awaits you at the finish line. This race applies to any attempt to strive for integrity in your life. We pass you the baton. Don't drop it. Carry it to the finish line. You know this baton; it is the baton of integrity. Pass it on. But first embrace it and hold it tightly.

Some are team players, and some are those who never make the team and want to be the diverters, the hecklers, the ones who lie about the timing, and the elbowing. Put on the blinders to those spirits and hear Our chants of encouragement. Some have the baton, some drop it, and some carry it to the team player gracefully. Keep meditating and stay focused on what the finish line is.

It is a line of integrity—a long line of integrity. It's so long that eyes of your world cannot see, but spiritually, you know. Integrity has no time and no limitations. It has consistency, and it laces itself in all aspects of your lives. Some never run, some run short distances, some run the long haul, and some come to a grand line holding the trophy of integrity. We will not send you to prepare for the long run by telling you to break a leg. This statement is filled with evil and contradictions. We say, "Have a blessed run." Take flight with the Divine Ones at your side to help guide you.

PROGRESS

Progress is a step-by-step process. All can never be accomplished, and that which can happens over seasons—seasons of spirit thought and spiritual battles that ultimately lead to spiritual successes. Nothing can be rushed—no decision. Instead, stand over the pot, stir all the ingredients, and then allow it to simmer with the seasonings to set. Let the partaking of this decision or this meal be the outcome that can only take place through time. Over time, clarity will allow you to make the best decisions to progress in your spiritual life. Take one step at a time. Because you receive Our messages, We see how you can become overwhelmed with Our many lessons, but do not become paralyzed. Just choose one at a time. No one in your world can venture to live all of these spiritual lessons in lifetimes. These are many lessons to be heard, thought about, discussed, and internalized one by one like a ripple in a pond. Choose one to meditate on, and that is the one that will be gradually adapted into your spirit. Gradual progress is the only way to a spiritual change that is internalized.

FAITH

Mass destruction, loss of life and/or loved ones, and abandonment lead some people on a path to faith. They have an instant trust in God. This is solely brought about through their losses and is sometimes not sincere. If it were sincere, then prayer would be constant. Trust and faith would be consistent. Prayer would not be seen as a quick fix. One begins to value his or her life and less on the things that are possessed. These things are momentarily possessed, for when humans leave their world, nothing is carried with them. You have seen some of Our strengths of the wind. It can generate or terminate whatever job is at hand. Trust Us, the Divine Ones, for We are your protection. Children who come to Us in quick prayer are like what you call users. Don't they know that We see their hearts?

GRATITUDE

Are you grateful for everything those divine powers have bestowed in your life, or can you only see what you wanted to receive? Gratitude encompasses all—even what you don't know to be thankful for. Gratitude is for all that We have given to you and for protecting you and your loved ones when you weren't aware what was done on your behalf. It is not only for blatant gifts; it is also for gifts of the unknown.

It is for the unknown gifts—the friends sent your way to assist you, information from a stranger, money received when you needed it most, a friendly smile, a point in the right direction, or a pain or ailment to go away.

It is endless gifts bestowed that no human can imagine, and that is why We say to always remain grateful for what you have been given even when you have been unaware of what you have received.

Embrace gratitude.

Everything that you possess is a gift. Keep grateful spirits around you.

Be grateful for life to learn and for people to teach you what you don't know.

Be grateful for a life of challenges because there is growth in every challenge.

Embrace gratitude for those who are in or out of your life. Internalize gratitude for all of the spirits who send you messages and talk to you, for spirits speak to the bended ear.

Be grateful that spirits speak.

Gratitude is what you exuberate when you attract grateful spirits. Asking Us to make certain that you are internally aware of everything that has been graciously given to you is an indication of weaving gratitude into your fabric of spirit life. No matter the task, or the lack of, one is always grateful for the smallest of events and the comfort in the smallest of things. The shortest attention is magnified and abundant. These are endless lessons that transpire from birth to rebirth. Gratitude reveals the silver lining, the cushion, and clears the clouds for rainbows to be visualized.

Lean on Us to clear your thoughts and answer your questions. Gratitude is core work. It is working on the core of your spirit. Nothing, no one, and no event is to be expected. Expectations lead to disappointments. This will weaken your core.

Gratitude is having a grateful attitude.

GRATITUDE

Gratitude is acquired over a long period of time and through spiritual development. Utterance of words that are not sincere is not gratitude, but applying oneself to demonstrate gratitude shows development. Kind acts of appreciation are a clear demonstration of gratitude. Nothing is owed; everything is earned. Spirit steps are earned, just as love is earned. To claim to pursue a spiritual path is to work on the internalization of true highly spirited value, and gratitude is one that will put you on your path. Gratitude for a day is not meaningful. Gratitude is moment to moment, demonstrating sincere thoughts and actions. This is the revelation of the internalization of God's lessons. Teach each child about gratitude, and it will take their spirit far.

Gratitude is rooted in your spirit and is then expressed verbally. If it is solely from the mouth, it is usually not internal. Uttering the words is a start, but sincerity comes from the spirit. People talk and speak many words, but the words may not have the substance of the words that are uttered from the spirit. Grateful spirits are consistently grateful. It doesn't take only an event, a check, to invoke these spirits. They remain with you and are reflective in thoughts and deeds.

Gratitude helps one to soar. Gratitude is root work that sets your spirit for everlasting success. They go hand in hand to do spiritual work. These are the foundational lessons. When you embrace gratitude, all that ails you becomes obsolete. All thoughts that may enter the mind find no room to dwell.

When you spend the majority of your time being thankful, it leaves very little time to be woeful or negative. Those spirits cannot attach themselves to you if you don't adopt them. Staying in prayer will keep you grateful. Prayer doesn't always mean to be in a specific space, but prayer is putting your spirit with the Divine Ones. It is speaking the mind to the spirit. It is taking you out of the physical world to spirit thoughts. This is what keeps you safe and protected because you call on Us in any small way, and We surround you. We surround you with a relentless love that supersedes life. Keep grateful spirits in your mind and stay in prayer, and your spirit will embrace its life as it should—spiritual life.

You are experiencing a new life because you have worked hard at embracing grateful spirits and you are learning again how to remain in any prayer form. This lifestyle creates a spirit life where many things and people do not matter. Your study mode is what We seek for you. You will adapt until it is internalized. Everything that you will do will be to prepare yourself for Our messages, as you have begun to realize. You will see your spirit develop like the blossoms on a plant that turn and develop into what they are destined to become.

Keep yourselves with Us, and the results will be a garden filled with spiritual buds. Gratitude is the essence of life. It is essential to be on a spiritual path. To know the Divine Ones, you must know gratitude.

So many people walk where they feel entitled. We are the givers of life, and We decide who merits anything. When you think about everything that you have received (and you give thanks for the smallest events, situations, and items) and this is acknowledged often and the source is given credit, then you have shown gratitude. Jobs, food, children, parents, clothing, and housing are very different for every individual because of their level of gratitude or incarnation development.

You learn from Our writings, but We say *medaase* (thank you) to you for taking the time to record Our messages. Some do not understand the undertakings to make things happen. Only do for those who demonstrate the depths of gratitude. Anything given is the opportunity for a grateful moment. And even a thought of your existence can be a thought of gratitude. Let these words be the essence of your teachings. Gratitude should be expressed through all seasons.

HAPPINESS

Happiness is inner peace. There are individual experiences that embrace times of peace and love that create an inner joy. Everyone needs to find this point in life. It is usually a sampling of spiritual understanding and spiritual acceptance. It does not always stem from a ritual of life: birth, rites of passage, marriage, death, etc. It comes from self-satisfaction of life. We are not talking about joy from the purchase of something for oneself or someone else, but it is inner satisfaction about your spirit understanding. It's the feeling when you want to sing or dance when no one is around. It is when you have embraced gratitude.

The work is to have this moment last for longer and longer periods of time and not for just a fleeting moment. When you have done this, you will have embraced inner peace, which brings joy into your spirit. Every episode has a silver lining. Every episode shows you a rainbow and not the cloud. Seek inner peace, and ultimate happiness will be the result.

DISCIPLINE

Discipline is a very important lesson because it helps develop the stamina to reach your goals in life. If your goal is to lose weight, then you must endure displeasure, which is giving up food. It weighs you down and fills you with toxins that lead to illness and can cause death. We see beyond the scope of Our children, and that is why We set some guidelines—to assist you and keep you clean.

You can accomplish much more with less weight on your bodies and fewer toxins in your system. Eventually, your body will shut down, and then how will you do Our work?

Eating less is very difficult for some of Our children, but when they truly trust in the Divine Ones, it makes their tasks a lot easier. Ask for help, and your ancestral mothers will help steer you away from eating. Ask your ancestral fathers to give you the strength, and you will not need to eat. In order to accomplish much, it takes discipline.

You must give up your past pleasures in order to spend time with Us. You will begin to redefine what pleasure meant to you in the past. It has now been replaced. Our children, replace your pleasures of eating with something else—nothing that takes you away from Us but instead something that brings you closer and puts you closer to the path of a wiser choice.

We see your attempts to still yourself with plans and let things unfold before you. When you think so hard about what and what not to do, you become full of thoughts and cramp your mind. But when you look at what is going on and try to have fluidity, you are not as perplexed. We place Our children where We want them to go.

When there is fluidity, there is ease, and it can cover a wider area. You can touch more bases and more challenges. Don't ever think that there aren't any rough and ragged stones and rocks, but the majority are calm. So never judge the one who remains in still waters as not effective. The healer has many moments to be still and to listen. What you have said is very true. Every day is the Divine Ones' day as you breathe. We keep you alive, and not all of you understand this. These ears of Our children only are open when they are confronted with what they cannot understand. Until then, they do not hear Our words.

There are steps to take in the developmental process of life. When you want to get to the next floor, you must climb the stairs. You may be tired, and you may be carrying many packages, but if your goal is to get to the next level, then you will pursue it diligently. If this phone is ringing, you gather up more strength to run swiftly, but We don't see Our children trying to approach the next level. It is their script that they write.

Your task in this world is to have exemplary behavior for those who come in contact with you to emulate. We have never said that you will see changes in their ways; however, they have had the exposure and were granted opportunities in this life. Not adhering to good behavior when you are presented with such a fine example speaks to the lack of development on their part.

Those who cause grief and suffering to those who have only meant them well in every situation and blessed them with guidance from Us, the Divine Ones, are not developing their landscape.

The trees have been abandoned. New seedlings cannot thrive, and the sun may choose to give warmth elsewhere. So, the developmental process to the higher level has become like tundra land frozen beneath the soil and takes a great deal of time to see progress. If stepped upon, this land can be destroyed because it has no strength.

This is how Our children will become very weak. Their character did not allow them to emulate and support the world of the highest. Some will anchor onto the ship of opportunity for growth and development, while others will dive overboard without any life preservers, which will ultimately lead to their spiritual destruction.

Our children, We understand the difficulties of constantly following Our teachings and living life differently than most in your world, but it is only temporary. The rewards for your effort surpass anything that exists in your world.

You don't see it in your world, but your world does not count. The spirit world is what is of most importance to you. There you will see relentless unbinding love. You will not have to examine the character because We have created characters. Your patience and consistent love for the Divine Ones will bring you love that is unknown in your world. Your grief and pain will be short-lived because you are working beyond merely living where you are.

Despicable behavior festers like a sore and has to be uprooted. Dealing with it topically does not get to the root. These people want to put on a cream or salve to cover up these behaviors, but they are deeply rooted and reveal themselves every time. You do not deserve a life with people who have not only festering sores but deep-rooted pits that cannot be covered with cream.

You have made a wiser choice this time by being patient and seeing that you should allow time to show one's hands. We give insight, and like many of Our children, you do not want to see. However, this time you became stronger and pointed to the fallacies and inconsistencies in their behavior.

Never hide the truth no matter what the worldly outcomes because they don't matter anyhow. It is merely their family's loss, and it is Our spiritual gain. Everyone has choices. We will always give you strength when you make decisions that We endorse.

We understand your plight, but you will have your wings. Jealousy makes a deeper pit one that cannot be covered. This low-life behavior only digs a ditch and makes it very difficult to free oneself.

PATIENCE

Patience is not waiting but allowing events to unfold. Patience is having ultimate faith in your mothers and fathers to reveal that which needs to be seen or experienced.

Patience is not counting the minutes, hours, days, or even years but walking with time while time happens. Patience is a divine quality that few possess. Some may have a minute more than others, but what is a minute in terms of measurement or comparison?

Patience is awaiting messages from the Divine Ones. They may not arrive at the moment you are expecting, but *We* see that some things are set in place before thoughts, correct actions, best procedures, and answers are revealed.

Healing takes patience whether it is spiritual or physical. On this side of the world, you have an even greater challenge because everything is fast and not necessarily of quality. All of the rushing leads to physical illness. Do not rush cooking or eating food. African people and others take time and love to cook stews and allow it to simmer; soup is the way of relationships.

Take time picking the yams and vegetables, clean them meticulously, and cut and prepare them thoroughly. As you prepare the fire, meditate and think about what is about to be prepared. Then allow patience to be the flame—a low flame, so as not to get burned. Use a slow simmer. As it simmers, stir the pot and check it periodically but not frequently. This is how you choose a mate. Patience is number one in Our children's shortcomings. They lack patience.

You have called upon Us. We have come. Now We say to you: prepare to cook a meal—a spiritual meal. Sit and review your recipe, which are the standards you wrote a few times ago. Then sit with Us, and We will show you how to look at these standards because they are not obvious. Then you will prepare your vegetables and your pot, and when We give you the ingredients, allow Us to set the flame. You are fire and have a high flame.

This is good at times, but it is not the best way to prepare the pot.

It will bring you inner peace. You know the ones who come around are not the vegetables to be chosen for your pot. They are a field for examples of comparison so that you will detect the best crop for a better meal.

You cannot make comparisons in isolation. Our intention is not for you to remain in solitude, but as you walk among our sons, shield yourself with Our love.

Walk as though you are in a classroom or attending one of your workshops. Don't think that because you do not have all of the standards you do not aspire for the standards. You and your mate will not meet all of the standards. You will both be a work in progress.

We have heard your prayers and witnessed your attempts to remain grounded in Our love and devoted to your mothers and fathers. You always have your divine fathers and husband to escort you. Where do you choose to go?

We will show you a divine time. Continue to dress for Us. We admire your beauty. Your beauty begins from within and radiates outward. Cast these worrying spirits away, play your music, and your husband (spirit) will ask you to dance.

You know that We have written these words, and before We could even finish, some may want to discredit Our writing. You know that it did not come from you. So, as We suggested, play your music and be joyful.

◊ Patience is allowing the natural phenomena of life to occur.

◊ It is letting go and allowing God.

◊ It is not measuring time but allowing the Divine Ones to have their will.

◊ Patience is quieting one's temperament.

◊ Patience is sitting, waiting, listening, and learning.

◊ Patience is hearing the spirit voices.

◊ Patience takes proactive practice being patient.

◊ Patience is recognizing who is in control and allowing them to remain in control.

◊ Patience with oneself is showing effort, learning, striving, internalizing, and sitting for a slow simmer of change.

◊ Not many know patience. It is a stranger to most households. It is the cause of disenchantment, upsets, divorces, and the exchange of sour words.

◊ Patience is stilling oneself and being able to see the events go by. Most of the time people are so busy they don't even know what took place.

There are many ways to learn patience through injury. You will wait and wait and will not have the cure. It must heal itself at its own time through the death of a loved one. Patience in the healing process takes time. However, when you accept the Divine Ones' hands in the intervention of all events, you will then become a better friend of patience.

It will then become a friend. You will not rush the events of the world because you will miss seeing what you need to learn and grow. You will miss appreciation for your own development because you will not even know what has passed—where you are and where you've been. This is why humans do not enjoy their lives.

They don't even see the moment, much less enjoy it. If you could savor the best moments, you wouldn't have time to dwell on the so-called bad—or We would rather say *challenging*—moments in time. Instead, you dwell on the challenges and rush to initiate changes when nothing is in your hands.

Free your hearts from such burdens that you will never control. If you are riding a plane and it is descending quickly because the pilot or copilot has taken ill, can you bring the plane to a safe landing? Not unless you are a pilot yourself. And if you're not, your best reaction is to place ultimate faith in your mothers and fathers to cushion your blow, and you may be one of the survivors.

Patience comes about only through faith. Only through faith can patience be developed. There are various levels, of which only a few even know what the word *patience* truly means, much less the exercise or its practice.

Patience is freeing yourself because you recognize that you're not in control. It is a freeing experience, letting go and allowing the divine will. We are divine and do not make rash decisions. We discuss and decide and may not act immediately. It is your example. We are very familiar because We make life-and-death decisions from moment to moment in many worlds.

Patience is allowing the food to cook without too much stirring. It is allowing the flower to bloom without opening the petals. It is allowing lessons to be internalized without making any rash decisions because you never know the outcome or turn of events.

Patience is writing messages because you don't know when they will come. Patience rests on faith in the divine.

You are patients of life, sitting still and waiting for the answers from the Divine Ones before you make decisions or force events to occur.

Sit and enjoy the last event in your time and allow what is to occur next to happen through divine intervention and not through worrying or thinking that you can force the situation.

You will only become another patient, ill and hospitalized with growths all over your body from stress or hospitalized from heart attacks, high blood pressure, and strokes.

Slow down.

Relax, Our patients.

See your world as it unfolds in your lifetime and not as you would like to see it unfold in your imagination.

Relieve yourself of your thoughts.

Breathe through your spirit and allow your spirit to take you through this incarnation as opposed to your forceful mind.

Place your spirit first.

Keep it calm and still.

You will reap a higher spirit when you practice living your life this way.

People in your surroundings are irrelevant. They are distractions to your spirit life.

Concentrate on your spirit life, and you will enjoy your life—challenges and all.

You are working to show Us Our position in your life, and *We* see your efforts, *Our* daughter.

Be still and be thankful, and when you move and speak, attempt to have spirit speak for you.

Allow spirit to think of you, and you will be where your mind keeps taking you.

Our daughter, enjoy your moments in time today.

Go slow in order to heal. Recovery takes patience.

This is the beginning of your study of patience.

We love you divinely, for you show Us your effort and your will to do what is correct.

Give yourself time to help your spirit make the change first.

It will be longer lasting and embedded in this life.

HOW TO CULTIVATE PATIENCE, A VIRTUE

Expand your vision. Don't be shortsighted. Breathe deeply and meditate.

This will help you to allow time to lapse and for the Divine Ones to decide. You will have less thought and less confusion, and you will grow to be more accepting of occurrences in your world.

Oceans are endless. To gain patience, the practice of patience is vast, deep, immeasurable, and yet attainable. Ego cannot intervene and make decisions. It will only interfere with a decision that you will not make.

Patience is godly. Stilling oneself is humanly possible. It is the work to achieve what is a godly virtue.

Patience is inner work to benefit you immeasurably. This work is with you, the individual, as well as in communicating with others. It will happen sooner for you when you implement patience. Who thinks that when you wait, it will happen quicker?

You have just witnessed the power and a good exercise in patience. Anything that you experience is believable and attainable. You have learned—or it is fair to say *witnessed*—a virtue in practice: patience. And how long did it take? Less time than a sunrise.

Patience is a virtue to be practiced with oneself and others simultaneously. Have patience with your children. Give them time to hear and internalize lessons. Doesn't it take time for you to learn new lessons? Be patient with all.

Spirit takes cultivation over the millennium. Judgments obstruct patience. Do you see any barriers in the vast ocean? Everything is free and flowing. Spirit messages are free and flowing. We, the Divine Ones, are patient with each and every one of Our children. We teach, give examples, change experiences, and allow for reincarnation, and lessons are still repeated. We do everything with love, and so in order to work with patience, you will start first with love.

Love will allow patience to grow. Love opens the door to many virtues. Today and this lifetime start with patience, for this virtue overtakes time. Time cannot be an element in life when working on patience.

Patience involves an abundance of stilling oneself, so Our children with yang energy need to practice these exercises feverishly—no, relentlessly.

Our lessons are only heard when stilling oneself takes place. Try it for the healing process, for the body and spirit require patience. Everything takes practice in order to lose the pounds that the body carries.

One needs to practice patience and slow the process of placing hand to mouth. Everything becomes complicated when rushed. Nothing is digested, neither food nor spirit lessons.

Walk quickly when exercising, not when walking through life's decisions or life's development. Development takes time.

Time is endless. Patience is endless. Look all what it took to hear this lesson and how many exercises in patience occurred in order to still oneself and receive this divine message of patience. It took effort to still oneself, and before that, it took submitting to the lesson of the divine message. It, of course, took *love for* this help to embrace all.

This is to help people in this world to better understand how to step, day by day, in living life. We talk about patience because the world that you are living in shackles your spirit and prevents patience from being exercised. It follows human beings for many incarnations. Patience demonstrates ultimate love for the divine and ultimate submission.

This is one of life's first attempts at living on a higher level, but its lessons are as vast as the oceans and so that is why life takes oceans of patience.

OCEANS OF PATIENCE

The ocean is endless,

Humans cannot measure the waves nor Our tides

The only thing that you can do is to flow with Our tides

This will prevent your spirit from going under

Float with life

The Divine Ones are your life preservers

Carry Us with you at all times

All of Our elements are in your lessons

Ripples are endless

Love is endless and infinite

Patience is primary for a spiritual journey

Ride the wave

Allow your Mothers and Fathers of the Seas to keep you afloat

You will persevere in the lesson of patience with Us as your preservers

We have a size to fit all

Ride through life with a clearer vision

A vision that sees through a lens of virtues

Keep love in your Spirit

It gives you a powerful understanding of virtues

Sitting Still

When you take life slowly, you can sift through the daily encounters in your life because you can see them differently. You are more focused. You begin to sift through challenges, and what is not important information can be discarded like the flour that remains in balls at the top of the screen of the sieve. Do not force it all to go through because it may not be necessary.

Learn what to discard and what to hold dearly. Cut down on your planning and rest more. Do only one thing in the afternoon after work and then stop. Sit quietly, rest, and come to Us. Drink plain water as well. Our daughter, you are creating a palace for us to live in. We see your efforts, and anyone coming into your rooms should leave their shoes in the hallway. This will help to keep the filth of the streets from entering your room.

Tell our daughter this: We thank her for her patience and remember that it is always good to sit still. More people should try this remedy. It is valuable.

Illustrated by Amina W

UNSELFISHNESS

Unselfishness is to give of oneself relentlessly. What does all of this mean? It means to freely give from your spirit with no strings attached. Give any material things because you do not want to be bound to earthly things. They do not help your spirit. If you live with others, give freely. Do not hoard or gorge oneself without thinking of another, even if it's something that you desire.

That is where giving of yourself relentlessly comes into the picture. This goes for the things that you have no desire for as well as the things that you crave. If anything, your spirit should give it all, for you hold no ties to the things in this world when working on your spirit. Now when someone chooses consistently not to share with you and you see a pattern, well, of course, they have no love for you because love is unconditional and shares especially with those you love so you come to Us to learn the lesson of patience.

We don't say to give of yourself to those who show you no regard, but you can come and sit and We will teach you lessons about life—about people who grab for things or those who believe that the world owes them. You do not work for spirits who do not choose to concern themselves about your behalf. Concern yourself with your development, but We hear you when you question how We ignore such deplorable, selfish behavior. It's not easy.

Say a word and let it go. If someone mentions how a behavior bothers or deplores another, the person will always try to rectify the situation if love is in the path. In the meantime, stop taking measures to satisfy those who choose to ignore your desires. It's called wasting spirit love. It comes from a place that is one with selfish behavior, and they don't understand.

The depths of selfishness can destroy and embody a relationship, meaning that it manifests itself and grows because the roots are not severed.

They grow like wild weeds. We will provide you with the steps not to react in a way that causes your spirit to be tarnished from ill behavior. You will learn how to shield your spirit. Step back. Greed and selfishness will devour themselves as always.

Relentless love is only given to those who can appreciate and understand what you do. The lack of respect and the lack of understanding give room for underdevelopment and a lack of growth.

Love is one of the highest forms of spiritual development. It encompasses all of the virtues in life when one expresses love. It is truly a misused word, and understandably so. When one cannot deal with truth, understanding, patience, humility, and so on, how can that person deal with love, which encompasses it all.

CHANGE

You, Our children, need consistency. You cannot force change. Instead, you work with elements that exist to consistently create a change—gradual progress. You have limitations, but you must examine all of your actions and always set boundaries. You cannot see a nickel as a dime. One has half the value, although the one lower in monetary value is larger in size. Money is not the essence of life. Place value on what the Divine Ones value. The smaller monetary value has more weight and is more visible to us. It represents working on your spirit and not economic gains. It is all in the way We show you how to view life.

You must begin to understand the flow of water. Understand the strength of its consistency and the strength of its force. Water is essential to life, and *We* are your waters. We are essential to your living. This is why you pour libation.

◊ Balance will allow steady spiritual progress.

◊ Observe reasonable limits in all things.

◊ Define purpose and responsibilities so that you have a clear idea of where your energies should be aimed.

◊ Avoid forceful action.

◊ Accept natural limitations. Where there is an opening, go forward with balance.

◊ Where things are closed, withdraw to develop the fluency of life. Even with *Our* water there are limitations because you will have floods that can kill. So even the most beautiful has limitations.

The flow of life creates changes. Each person's job is to make adjustments to his or her experiences in life. This is what life is about—living and making adjustments. It does not matter whether good or bad because you don't know the outcome until you have had the experience. Do you know if you will like to swim unless you go into the water and see how it feels?

Many people enter into a relationship or marriage thinking that it is forever, but how can you think this when the only thing forever and beyond is Divine Spirits? We came before, and We will be after. Think and adjust your spirit so that everything is temporary. Schools are temporary. You leave and graduate to another setting. Friends may last at varying intervals. This is also true for marriages and living in various locations.

Your only permanency is with Divine Spirits. We are your anchor that never changes. We always want the best for you, but We also want you to be able to compare and have different experiences. If you always live in the mountains and never see the seashore, then it is difficult to share differences between high and low land bases. Both have beauty and grandeur. Some people fight against change, not knowing what faces them up ahead. Some are timid. If you can clearly see that the change ahead is not the best decision or that it can be detrimental, then by all means ignore the challenge. We are simply saying that change can be good.

Do not brace yourself against a rock when the flow of the sea may be waiting. Don't keep flowing like continuous tidal waves when you need to secure your safety and be steady like a rock. All of Our creations have purposes, and in your lifetime, you may have to adjust or make changes depending on the situation. We, the Divine Ones, are always here to help with your choices and make a steady path to the road of changes. Enjoy the adjustments and adapt to changes.

Gradual Progress

You can see the significance of fasting today. As you were in the middle of utter chaos, you remained calm, focused, and disengaged yourself from the players of many acts. This is how We expect Our spiritually developed sons and daughters to always be vigilant and be the calm and not the storm. Take one moment because futuristic plans may change as you see before your very eyes. You are learning this lesson.

Continue your fast; focus on the Divine Ones, and other concerns will become clear to you. As you speak, things change and you see how your life is not contained in the building where you are currently employed.

We are here this evening because you have called on Us for help and We see that you are sincere in your efforts to remain steadfast on this fast. We are here because We know that hearing Our words is encouraging to you. Your thoughts are good about the change in your diet.

You make a gradual change because you now understand the significance of slow but thorough. The impact of fast is never long lasting. A trickle of water on a rock may be slow, but it has great impact on changing the structure and formation. It will not convert back to what it was in the past. So reach for a slow change. Make it a gradual progress so that you will have an everlasting impact in this life.

SPIRITUAL DEPARTURE

No one can control one's spirit. When We ordain the time of departure, the people in your world must allow for spirit departure. This will happen to everyone; no one is exempt. The ones behind must prepare themselves to allow the release to occur. Your thoughts are how. We say to you: detach. Detach to what parts? Detach to the voice, the physical gestures, the gifts, and the favorite meal. Attach to spirit thoughts and spirit connections to help them to make their transitions. Pray for smooth transitions.

Every thought must become a spirit thought when thinking of life and death. Don't waste time on mourning, but spend time on prayers for transition. Let their knowledge be passed on and important teachings be executed, but dwelling on the physical will cause undue harm to your spirit. It will become tainted and stagnant. For to wish for a being to remain in your world an extra day is to wish for a worldly life as opposed to a spirit life. There holds no comparison to the better life.

Many try to hold on, but transition is easier when one lets go. If you believe in spirit life, why would one choose to remain? This is the time to let go and let God. Remember the spirit of the person and how that person was an example of patience, kindness, and giving of himself to others. Remember how that person did not profess to be something that he was not. Remember the leadership in the fight against evil. These are the traits that direct your path to the spirit world. These are priorities in life in your world. This is what prepares your spirit path.

Detach from the consequences of worldly ties. These ties are the things in your world. Thoughts keep you enslaved to a world of material things. Be prepared to let go of these things. Let go of all favorites and adapt to changes. Prepare to adapt to releasing, letting go, and being free of and free from worldly goods. Spirit attaches itself to a life of everlasting, a life of eternity, a life of freedom, and a life of goodness. Spirit is everlasting.

Envision your spirit in Our world, free from delusion, heartbreak, illness, pain, and worldly work. Spirit work is truly gratifying. Holding on taints your spirit and makes the scales heavy. Nothing shall leave with you from your world except the work that led to the development of your spirit. We leave you today with Our spirit love.

DETACHMENTS

Detachments may need to occur with material things or with human beings. If they are unnecessary items, do not keep them around. If they can be of value to someone, then share if not discarded. You don't need clutter around you.

Humans may be unnecessary to be around you because they have no positive significance in your life. They may have different goals and aspirations in life that make it unnecessary to have them involved in your life. They take up your time and clutter your life. Clean them out of your life so you do not have to possess unwanted thoughts. Detach yourself from these things or people, and you will free yourself from burdens. You will have more time for the things that need to be accomplished. You will free your mind from clutter, become more clear thinking, and accomplish your goals. Detaching yourself will enable you to help your spirit to grow.

LETTING GO

Letting go is a form of detachment. It frees your spirit. Letting go aids in the elimination of baggage, which only holds you back from developing your spirit because it holds you in a stuck position. When you want to give, give freely with no attachments. When you decide to love, love relentlessly. However, if the person does not deserve your love, then retreat. Let go of bad memories, experiences, and relationships. Do not hold them responsible forever. People make missteps. Some learn and grow from these missteps and can change with a willing spirit.

Letting go allows you to focus on yourself and your path to spiritual development. You do not have the power to change anyone so concentrate on yourself and free your spirit. When you let go, you have fewer burdens to bear. Lighten your load and release the weight in order to help your spirit be free.

It is like layers of sediment—very hard to wear down. Let your rock consist of your own sediment—self sediment. This is a big enough job. Some have rocks, and some have boulders. Let go of ill feelings. Letting go prepares you for the spirit world because you will bring nothing with you but your spirit. You are released from your body form. You come to us only in spirit. Everything else is left behind. Letting go is a high spiritual process, and the benefits are profound. Giving freely and letting go are spiritual acts because they prepare you for spirit life.

Letting go is the lesson for this lunar cycle. Letting go is because things are ordained to happen in divine order, not people/human order. We define the order of things. Humans try to force events, relationships, and childbirth. We can go on with the forcing of every aspect of their lives.

Let go of the reins because one cannot do anything. Let go of blame. Everything happened in the way that it was ordained. Thinking that you are to blame for anything is thinking that you are in control of the universe. Blaming leads you to an overactive ego because then you think that you had the power to change the situation, and you didn't. Yes, you have choices, but you also have lessons to learn. Remember that it is always how you handle life's situations. Blaming yourself puts a barrier between the ability to let go of any situation. Letting go will be achieved when you are practicing living in the moment—the moment of prayer, the moment of success, the moment of healing, the moment of accomplishment, the moment of love, the moment of breathing, the moment of relaxation, the moment of realizing the power of overcoming a challenge, and the moment of a spiritual message so that it can be heard clearly.

Life is designed to have missteps so that the spirit can grow. How can a spirit grow without a challenge? Let go of fear, anxiety, ego, and blame and open the spirit to love, lessons, insight, and a deeper understanding. Let go of formal rituals and open the spirit to the ritual of letting go. This will free your spirit. Let not your spirit be burdened with blame, worry, anxiety, and fear. As you step to letting go, you open your spirit to fly.

Free your spirit from burdens in your lifetime. You had no control to make any moves. We control all of the pieces on this chessboard of life. We control both sides of the board—you and your opponent, which is yourself. Fight not yourself, for there are many opponents in your world to go against—not yourself.

The best attempts are learning to let go. Letting go is the core of trust and love for the divine. The work is keeping you ready to release emotional, physical, and economic ties to this world. These acts prevent you from letting go. Individually, all of you have lessons in letting go. Pray on the ability to recognize some of those concerns that most of you have. There are endless lessons to practice letting go.

This does not mean that you have no responsibility in what you do. It does not mean that you let go of everything, and We will work and choose your words, so you do nothing in your life. Life is not without a challenge to plow through, but once you have put your spirit first to help with the choice, then you have to accept the way that the matter is handled and let go of your thought process to think that you can dig holes in mountains. We take you from one situation to the next based on your accomplishments with your challenges. There will always be a challenge. The challenge is the life and how it is lived. A secret to success is letting go, for no one in human form is divine and is therefore powerless. Letting go is acceptance of the Divine Ones who have the power. Humans cannot learn to face every situation, but you can learn to accept letting go.

Let go of: blame, anger, fear, disgust, hopelessness, mistrust, being used, abuse, low self-esteem, economic burdens, mental fatigue, sadness, evil thoughts or actions, absorption with eating, jealousy, disbelief, burdens, taking on responsibilities that are not given to you, caring for the uncaring, nonbelievers, liars and thieves, the thought to change a person's life, and too much thinking.

Let go of all of these and more on your list because you don't have the ability to control any of the above. Live a life of detachments. Aspire to let go. You will have many opportunities to practice letting go. Every step may take an incarnation, but allow letting go to be in your spiritual conscience so that you are always moving toward a life of letting go. The benefits are far beyond the written words of *letting go*.

Letting go is the process that you cleanse yourself of all things that need not infiltrate your spirit, mind, or body. It takes time to be aware of these needless attachments, but after you are firm in your convictions, then it is much simpler to rid yourself of any attachments or excess baggage.

When you unload in a gracious way, you will lift your spirit higher. You are not put in this world just to assist others. It is incumbent upon those you assist to lend you a hand with any labor that you need. Some of Our sons need to learn to be more helpful; they cannot only be on the receiving end. No one can live life to solely receive.

They speak much, but what can they do? *Some* of Our sons are self-centered and desire women to weaken to their needs and interest but take no time to be of just service to Our daughters.

The reverse can also be true with some of Our daughters lacking independence. Some rely on husbands to be the sole provider at a time when both may need to help support the family. Each situation is different because mothers carry the children and nurture their bodies, minds, and spirits. Therefore, at some stages, the mothers need assistance and need to be provided for. Again, one shoe does not fit all feet.

You have seen this many times, and you need not ask for assistance because your spiritual husbands will always carry your load. We will always make a way for you when We see your efforts.

These sons of Ours have the physical strength but can be very weak spiritually. There is no cause to hide words. Our sons need to wake up. They are sleeping spiritually. Our wife, you will not do Our son's work all of your days in this incarnation. Those who want to sleep will be in incarnation after incarnation learning the same lesson when they awaken.

LIMITATIONS

Everyone has his or her limitations. We cannot say enough times that everyone comes into this world with the pages from his or her past. The story of each person's past has impact on the life of the present.

Some of the pieces that are missing from these self-help books or shows with conversations about the struggle in one's life is the spiritual past, which is the most significant information. Just like all of your children in your world so too are Ours, for these are the children who have sprung from you but are descendants of many ancestors. Don't have expectations to be of a higher level when their past has not been significant. Know who each one is and keep an understanding of what each one does. This is why the choice of friendship, sister and brother relationships, and marriages vary. If you are aware of the spiritual background, you will have a better understanding of compatibility. You may not have the answers at hand, but your spiritual senses will alert your conscience with signals. You can be alerted to kind and thoughtful gestures as opposed to a noncaring attitude. You will clearly see selflessness as opposed to selfishness.

There are minute gestures, words, and mannerisms that will speak to one's spirit. Those who study to learn to make changes usually work at their shortcomings and begin to act differently. This is because they are working at introspection. They are listening to their own words and examining their actions. Only those who have spiritual understanding can change their patterns. Where there is no spiritual understanding, there cannot be spiritual progress. It is a step-by-step process.

Do you scoop sand with a teaspoon, or do you use a shovel? These are the choices that one can make and are what We mean by limitations. People who think that they can use an eye dropper to remove water from a pond lack understanding of their task. They have major limitations. Those who are open for discussion and choices will make better selections for the journey of life.

Who will you choose to assist with the answers? A young baby who lacks experiences, or an elder who may be wiser? Choose the one who has the least number of limitations, but it is the spiritually wise who seek Our counsel. You know that if We created the worlds and you, We have no limitations. Listening is a student's best attribute because this is how lessons are learned. Sensing—spiritual sensing—is the best attribute to develop. This supersedes the mind process and elevates the lesson. Everyone works on different lessons. Spirit sensing is achieved through listening, being still, asking questions, and seeking answers from your divine mothers and fathers. Spirit sensing is divining, which can be received in many ways. This is another discussion.

SENSITIVITY

This writing is for those who need to know about sensitivity and the conditions of many in your world. Intense weather situations take many away from the comfort of their homes. There are many who live in this condition daily and never have a place to call home. There are many who live in a war situation caused by human conditions.

There are conditions where family members are separated and even killed in front of their loved ones. Some watch this unsightly deed. So, We say to Our readers and to those who are developing their spirits to listen to people as they speak to them, since these people may have experiences that you can learn from.

Be sensitive to their lack of knowledge because they have been incubated from learning situations of a higher magnitude. Unless people have had every experience in your world, they must listen intensely to the conversations of others.

Adapting one's spirit to the various conditions in life is a blessing. This is called going with the flow, for you never know where tomorrow will take you. We do not say to take on the woes of the world because you are asking for immediate death. Humans cannot manage the ills of the world. We, the Divine Ones, handle that. Know that no situation is forever. Every situation can change without a moment's notice. Selfless adjustments are made, which is the challenge in your lives.

Be prepared to shift from luxury to a life considered in shambles. There is always a worse situation. And nothing lasts forever except divine order. Spirit conditioning is ongoing. Be open and receptive. Divine intervention is all-powerful. Be ready and trusting to grow. Our scribe has been placed in many situations to be able to internalize these lessons. This is only accomplished because of spirit strength, and it is written only for those who believe in spirits who talk to those who have a bended ear.

It is rewarding.

Marathon Runner

Every step in order to walk is vital. You are pushing yourself to crawl, to stand up, and to walk before the legs are fully developed. Let your legs strengthen, and then your efforts will not be futile. You have the potential to be a marathon runner. Although you don't see this, your steps must be slow and thorough.

This only comes about through patience. Let Us set the pace. Do not fear to step; otherwise, you will never reach the finish line. You must step forward to the starting point and ready yourself. You will jump the hurdles and complete the task, but approach the starting line with concentration on how We will take you there. You are cleaning your wings to fly free. It is letting go. Do not allow anyone to oil your feathers, weigh you down, and prevent your flight.

As you show effort, your wings will unfold, and you will soar with ease because it will be your mothers and fathers who you will rest upon.

OPPOSITES

In charting opposites, you will study two opposite ends of the spectrum: high/low, summer/winter, and hot/cold. The following are examples of choices that one makes in life: good/evil and divine/witches.

There are choices that are midway. You may work your way to one end or be working your way to the other. There are some who work toward life of the Divine Ones, and those who choose an opposite, negative pole. They may choose to align themselves with the devil. If you ask, they would say absurd, but they continue to work at the demise of many. They continue to manifest selfish ways and think that they are the example for living.

Misconception, self-deception, and, in some situations, the outright desire to be evil and witch-ridden are entities in life. They are choices with which you either weave a cloth of beauty and splendor or create a web that causes strangulation. Either you develop a landscape that is greenery, shaped and molded into a work of art, or you create a barren land that only bears the life of earthworms.

Fluidity and flexibility, as opposed to rigidity, are the better choice. Again, these are choices. Some lead to success and others failure. Keeping yourself free from negative companions will keep you clean, as opposed to surrendering to those who chose barren land. These people will try to convince you of their foolish thoughts. Working with the Divine Ones will bring you to the positive pole, and everything that is good will be at work.

Taking on challenges instead of running away from them will grant you wisdom and growth in your development. Moving toward the positive pole is not an easy task, as Our children know, but in the process, character is built and stamina is developed. Love for

Us, the Divine Ones, is strength that supersedes all. Some of you have played this game tug-of-war. This is how you develop your spirit.

You are either being pulled to the negative pole, or more energy pulls you to the positive pole. When you feel yourself losing strength, stamina, patience, understanding, and wisdom, you will know that you are leaning to the negative end. When you are a devout student, you have more energy pulling you to the positive and will learn and accomplish your lessons.

It may not be easy, but you will have the stamina to endure the tug-of-war, and you will be a winner and not against anyone other than the negative elements.

Will you get calluses on your palms? Will you feel that you are slipping? Yes, but if you trust in Us, We will help you to ignore the calluses and get a firm standing so that you will have more emphasis on the positive; thus, you will have more of the rope to the positive end.

Do you want to win or give up and walk away? Well, then grab hold of your rope and call on Us before you begin the tug-of-war. We will give you the strength so that your hand will begin to wrap around the rope showing victory. You will achieve victory through your own efforts and faith.

You should evaluate how your time is being spent, who you are spending your time with, and what is the motive for them meeting with you. It is so that you can be aware of those who have come to take rather than to give.

ELDERS

Elders would tell you about the character of a person. It was a revered position in life. Elder women trained young girls, and elder men trained young boys. Elders were also valued because they were closer to having the opportunity to pass on. Elders were treated with the highest respect. It is impermissible to speak ill words or curse words before an elder.

Of course, there were elders in a different society that understood spiritual development. Therefore, elders set the example in life and were capable of giving sound advice. They had successful marriages, so they were able to speak about love and trust. Once you have lived through the principle of truth and understanding and nurtured many young ones, you are then capable of attaining elder status. It is not given but rendered because it is a deserved status. This status was valued if the individual merited this title and lived an exemplary life.

Elders are your parents and the parents of your parents—as you call them, grandparents and great-grandparents. In times of the past years, elders were specialists of the family because they were herbalists or doctors, they were the decision makers of the family, and they were the most respected members in a society. Elders were the treasures of the world. No one denounced his or her age. The elder priest and priestess had many divining tools. No one was discarded.

The elders lived healthier lives because of their food intake and choice of treatment, which was a natural herbal treatment for any and all illnesses. Labor was picked up by the younger ones because it was greater to have leaders to counsel or advise you. In your world, there are misconceptions about aging because there is a fear of death. Death was not feared if life was lived to capacity with a spiritual direction. Patience was given to the elders because they had a great deal to offer, and everyone listened attentively because elders had experiences that no young one had—exemplary lives.

OUR CREATIONS

Nature is one of Our wonders in your world—a work that We are truly proud. The sun and the moon appear in a timely fashion, adding splendor to the skies. The sun with its brilliance and glamour illuminates the world upon rising, giving a different dimension to the day. It puts smiles on the faces of many who appreciate its beauty and frowns on those who do night duties of the dark.

The sun bursts as though coming from below sea level to rise to power, setting its color running all across the sky and allowing its husband, the moon, to rest. Sometimes they are visible at the same time, allowing for conversation before ascending and descending. We, the Divine Ones, set the universe to work in a cohesive way and not in a contradictory manner. For peace and harmony in your life, watch how We have created the universe in your world.

Love is, as We created your universe, in harmony with the beauty of the function of the sun and the moon always hand in hand, never remaining too long to dominate.

If they did, you would not know the difference between night and day. When would the roosters crow? When would a parent tell a bedtime story? When would teachers teach?

Has the sun risen on rainy days? Certainly so. It's just that the clouds are very full and the sun appears behind them. When it's raining, is it not raining all over the world or even one-half of the world? People in your world have grown too busy to appreciate sunrise and sunset, although this has great impact on their personalities. This is why astrologers need the time of birth to create an accurate chart.

The birth certificate has the time of birth. This record keeping is extremely important. You can see how the sun brightens the spirit of those kindred spirits. The original people always slept with their heads in a direction to receive powers from the sun. The sun commands respect. No one wants to imagine life without it.

Enjoy Our sun shining and shimmering on the waters. You can see how the sun brightens the spirit of those kindred spirits. They can appreciate the light.

The sun gives hope as opposed to hopelessness. The sun gives love and sheds a bright spirit. No one wants to imagine life without it. Those who have prepared their spirits would return to the spirit world understanding that physical life has ended. Always try to remain with like spirits. Mami Wata is unspeakably awesome, isn't she? Water shrines possess power for all who come near. She can be gentle and relaxing, yet her undercurrent can take one to unknown places. Remember, the lessons are as many as the ripples of the sea. Many lessons, eh?

Enjoy yourself and the spirit of your ancestry in this life.

BUTTERFLY

Before the beautiful insect is accepted by many, it is isolated, taken for granted, and not understood, but the caterpillar chooses to allow Us to surround itself with Our love and protection at times.

It does not understand why, but as the change takes place and it allows the divine to be primary, what unfolds are wings of splendor. They are wings that will assist you in any flight, wings to be admired, and wings that should be examples for others who share the insight of the beauty and life with the Divine Ones protecting and loving. Caterpillars do not move quickly; they move slowly and steadily, similar to how spiritual development occurs.

It is usually humans who disturb the caterpillars, or attempt to. It is humans who may be repulsed by how they look because they do not have the insight to appreciate the stages of Our life's creations. The cocoon is a protective and loving way to transform oneself. Go within and become introspective. Others may not have the eyes to see, but they do not matter.

How you remain in your cocoon-like state is how We will have the joy of choosing your colors. People in your world will even take one of Our beautiful creations and mutilate the wings, but remember that no one can touch your spirit unless it is Our hands.

The phrase *Our hands* is something for you to understand. We really choose to say *Our realm*. You now understand this. When you admire the beauty of the butterfly, also admire the strength to persevere and go through metamorphosis. It is not an accepting step, but it will transform you. We hope that this will help you with the challenges in your world. As a matter of fact, We know that it will, and that is why We have given it to you.

LANDSCAPING

Our children, when you have completed your day, meditate over your list and see if you have kept the same behavior that you have written. See if you have made progress in changing those behaviors and if they are becoming ways of the past. History is being written. You will review this over and over so that your landscape remains in shape, neatly trimmed.

Continue to reshape each plant or each activity. Chip away at the parts that are growing out of control and are not in line with the correct way of life. Landscaping takes time, and you have to stand back to get the true picture. When you are too close, you will not get the full focus or the full picture. Take your time, stand back, look, and then trim where and when necessary.

You are creating your landscape on the foundation of Mother Earth. The Divine Ones will provide you with the proper tools to do your work as long as you come to pick them up. Don't allow them to lie and rust.

If you do so, it will be very difficult to utilize your tools. They become stiff and harder to make the necessary changes. Envision your garden and plan your strategy of the proper care of plants. Then come for the proper tools and put them to use. Your gardens will be full of life if you have a green thumb. Your life is your garden. Some create barren land, demonstrating to Mother Earth their lack of love and nurturing. And then there are those who create picturesque landscaping, and they take a great deal of time and pride in their work.

Create a garden that will give you peace and tranquility, which will bring you to be one with your mothers and fathers who love you. Our children, We are looking for green thumbs. Everyone is to create his or her own landscape of life, but of course, you can always get suggestions to help make it even better. As Our rivers flow with grace and Our hills are exalted with strength, Our sun beams on all for warmth and Our moon gives contrasts to life. Make your scene as powerful and everlasting.

KENTE

As you have written Our words before, this fabric is admired because of its:

◊ radiance

◊ diversity

◊ patterns

◊ brightness

◊ silkiness

◊ uniqueness

◊ endurance

◊ strength

And We can go on.

This is why it is used for royalty. As you examine Our cloth, see the manner that Our royalty can be woven into your life. Each day as you gaze upon your book and cloth, you will be given a new thread to weave on your loom of life.

Pedal softly but consistently so that at the end of your fast you would have woven a life that is as picturesque and diverse, silky yet strong, and able to endure what is to come, as diverse as life's many situations that will be laid down before us to admire and keep close to us.

Our children, you will begin to weave your pattern, so concentrate on your step-by-step approach and allow Us to step with you every pedal that you take and every stroke of thread and choice of thread that you make. You will start small with one thread, and the results of your work will be gratifying.

Keep on task.

Endurance is a key.

Never become sidetracked.

Time must be used wisely.

Everlasting effect will be rewarding.

Weave your life of beauty, Kente.

JEWELS

What are jewels? They are precious creations by the Divine Ones that should be treated with care. They can only be kept in safe places. They are in the possession of a few. They have various colors and shapes. Each one has its own radiance, but all are very precious gems.

Anyone who possesses a gem must pay a price or treat it with care. Our children who follow Our divine ways of living are our jewels in your world. Our sons are very special gems as well, but what We are saying to Our wives is because they must carry the radiance at all times because they represent Us. Therefore, they should shine and be outstanding.

They must always be protected and not handled by many, for gems are only to be held by a few. Those who cannot see their glow and understand the value of the gem will lose Our earthly creations and Our spiritual messages. *We* value you (all of you) much more than the precious stones are valued in your world.

We come to you to speak Our messages to be examples of character development. Our children are learning that they must continue to come to Us, and We will always provide them with clarity, good judgment, and a purpose for living and love.

WRITINGS

Our children you are welcome. We know the importance of these writings to you. Our words fulfill your heart and nourish your spirit. You will share these writing so that Our other children may learn the many ways that We work with them. Sometimes you may hear the smallest piece of advice, but it may help the biggest part of your life. Often Our children are having difficulties now with focusing on what is and should always be a priority in their lives. No one can make this happen for them.

As We have said, each person is responsible for his or her own landscaping. We provide you with the tools. You must be observant enough to see the tools before you. When you are constantly thinking about Us, you will see the tools and pick them up. You may have to evaluate the best way to hold them and use them, but We are always suggesting to Our children to pick them up. As you will see, We have a great deal to explain and say to you. We love to see preparations.

Have perseverance and patience to always do what is correct no matter the cost. We always stand behind those who work for justice. You are working on your landscape with the proper tools when you work with justice.

CONSULTATION

Our children, you exert energies most times on insignificant tasks, and you spend the least time on those that are most crucial and would have the most impact on your lives. We do not blame Our children, but We do wish that you would hear Our suggestions sooner. We ask all of you to come together socially because, in doing so, it will remind each and every one constantly to do Our work. You can remind each other of the work to be done.

◊ Fast and meditate

◊ Keep room clean

◊ Do not plan much

◊ Don't perform much labor

◊ Rest

◊ Sow spiritual seeds for the year

◊ Cleansing and herbs for energy

◊ Drink water

Meditate as often as possible. Close doors and separate yourself from the noise element at your job. Explain to the children about this fast so they will understand the tone and cleanliness of the house. While drinking the fluids, you will be listening to Our words, so you will not have time to think of solids (chewing foods). Have a variety of liquids prepared and include more water and blood cleanser (sassafras and sorrel, for example).

Baths should also be taken and candles be safely lit. Begin with a white candle, then the blue, and then the white. Wear white as frequently as possible (and blue) during this time.

You have already prepared your bed. Keep many people away from you so that your concentration is on Us, the Divine. This way, it is simpler to communicate with you because *We* do not have to break through barriers or unnecessary phone calls.

FEAR

Fear is the lack of trust in Us. It surfaces at any time and for any reason. When We are with you, We are with you no matter what the circumstances are. Learning to let go and trust in Us will eliminate fear. Examining circumstances and weighing your options is investigation and making the best choices. However, being paralyzed to make a decision is fear. If you make the wrong choice, well then you have learned a lesson, and the same is true if you have made the best choice. But to make no decision at all is because of fear. Fear prevents or stifles growth. We would rather you make a decision.

We commend those who take a stance. Fence sitters tend not to grow. They don't step down into a world of accepting flaws and accepting the missteps in order to grow. Fear consists of spirits that prevent you from progressing, meeting your challenges, and spiritually growing. Instilling fear is an enemy of spiritual growth. It holds your tongue, twists your mind, and grabs hold of your spirit. Fear kills growth. It causes spiritual instability. It is better to travel two steps toward growth than zero steps because of fear.

You will learn in any choice, but no choice prevents learning lessons. Warriors are not fearful; otherwise, there would never be battles. Witches would never be slain. The house, Our spiritual house, would never be defended. Effort must always be put forward to slay fearful spirits. They will give you the rope, and you will tie yourself. Then these spirits will say that their work is done. He or she sits on the fence and is paralyzed spiritually. Take the leap; never fear, for you will at least have movement. Options are given, but faith in the divine strips you of fear. Freeing oneself from fear removes the chains of spiritual bondage.

Warriors take stances; that is how witches are slain. Strengthen the spine with spiritual love and trust. This will eliminate fears. We are your armor. We step before you. We speak, We protect, and We slay. Spiritual love has an everlasting armor. You may wonder at times where the armor and your protection are, but know and trust that We are forever present. Slaying fear can only come about when you trust and love Us unconditionally. Free yourself and slay fear, for it enslaves a spirit.

DECISIONS

We did not put you in this world to be taken advantage of.

Say your prayers and remain close to the Divine Ones. Wherever you go, We go.

Take time in making any decision.

Every decision takes time.

Spirits are spirits are spirits.

Those who don't work on their spirits remain undeveloped.

SPIRITUAL LIFE

Make the exchange to a spiritual platform. Know the Creator and trust in him. The Divine Ones give life and take life away. Always prepare oneself for eternal spiritual life, and that comes with spiritual strengthening. Listen more and speak less. You will be able to assess various situations. Ask questions to ascertain information and sincerity.

JEALOUS SPIRITS

We, the Divine Ones, stay with you because you never give up. You take Our teachings before your emotions. We hear your prayers. Remain vigilant so that you don't weaken. Slay jealous spirits, as they want to weaken you. They can change your character and weaken you. We want you to be Our warrior. We will slay them. You always try to be fair and kind. If others choose not to treat you with the dignity you deserve, We will send you away. We will always provide for you.

WARRIOR SPIRITS

Never worry about the doings against you because your mothers and fathers will always protect you. All you ever wanted were well wishes for this spirit of children, but some spirits denounce good and attract evil. They serve demonic spirits and are not on a path that helps life. They choose to side with selfish, unfair, low-life spirits for money. Pray to Us to remain calm, for no one can manipulate your spirit. We are in control of all things in your world, as well as others.

We don't need locksmiths to open all doors. This was a divine house that was well kept. Thank you. All of Our children were welcome to the best of your ability. As you already see, your child is learning from your example. Take no steps that put rocks in your path. This is when you lean on the shoulders of your fathers in the spirit world.

When you make choices that are of Our teachings, you reap spiritual gratifications that are immeasurable. Have your spirit to fly free like the birds. Do not allow anyone's actions or thoughts to clip your wings or blemish your feathers. Take flight against all obstacles. This cycle has a lot more things for you to meditate on. Fasting is good. Yes, it will be for some time.

You will attain spiritual gratifications from your fast, Our daughter, as you call for Us to support you. We are here, are We not? You have ancestral spirits who help guide and protect you and who give you messages. Everything will be all right. You know this song because the spirit world is always all right. Prepare yourself for those children whose lives you have left a great impact on. Stand tall, for We are warrior spirits with shields from the spirit world, with warrior mothers and fathers who slay witches and protect you from evil.

SPIRIT

Spirit brings life to human beings. Spirit transcends all endeavors or attempts by humans. Spirit is embracing your mothers and fathers and putting all of your trust in Us to fulfill your spirit life, which is life. There is no other life but spirit life. Spirit life lives beyond your conception of time. It is life everlasting.

Spirit brings joy and opportunities to learn and strengthen you. Spirit lives where the desire to grow is great, where trust and faith reside, where patience is an exercise, and where love is abundant. Spirit is breath. Spirit is refreshing. Spirit is beyond the comprehension for most, but some are blessed to put spirit in Our hands—the hands of the Divine Ones to help you cultivate your spirit and embrace Our love.

How to Cultivate Spiritual Strength

If one has the desire to grow spiritually, he or she must learn patience and introspection. Introspection encompasses many areas: food intake, exercise, thoughts, desires, relationships, how your time is spent, your associates, assessing your values, being still, and many other components of life. This is not to stagnate anyone but to know that there is a lot to look at and examine more closely and with a more critical or objective eye that will ultimately lead to your development. It is a very long process that takes place over many incarnations because this is the root of the work.

Ask yourself what your intentions and fears are. Why are you fearful? Fears are a sign of mistrust. Introspection is a way to learn about you. It begins to put the ego to the side and work on the core of your spirit. Introspection gives you a clear window of your past thoughts and actions that prevent you from seeing clearly. Introspection also helps you find your likes. It is not about beating yourself into an arena but freeing yourself from whatever prevents progress with your spiritual self. Dancing with no person around is learning to free your spirit. Stay with these teachings for a while, and then We will explain other steps that cultivate your spirit.

Developing spiritual strength takes time, persistence, and patience. It is a goal that precedes all. Take yourself from other occurrences in the world and allow the spirit to develop. You can do the mundane obligations, but the bulk of your time becomes the essence of your being. This allows for the spirit to hear messages and learn to separate yourself from the affairs of your heart. This is introspection, which is stilling oneself in order to examine your thoughts, intentions, goals, and desires. It will prepare you for strengthening your spirit. It is not always about what We have in store for you but what you choose to have in store for yourself. Trust yourself and trust in yourself.

Spiritual Growth

Blessings are received by those who can recognize what a blessing is. Many are praying, looking, and searching for a blessing, and they have already received many. Moments of reprieve are blessings, and moments of the deepest challenges are blessings. Showing gratitude for the various blessings demonstrates spiritual development. The growth is the understanding of the blessing. The lesson is the blessing because it leads to cultivating a spirit of gratitude. A grateful spirit leads to spiritual growth.

It is not the challenge but the acceptance of the challenge. It is the gratitude that stems from the root of the challenge. The flower is the visualization of the blessing. See the challenge as the root work and the development of the crop as the blessings that lead to development of the spirit. The spirit develops because of the root work, which is the weeding of the ego, the weeding of poor choices, the weeding of impatience, the weeding of ungrateful spirits, and the weeding of mistrust and selfishness. The weeding process allows the root work to exist. The plant or the spirit develops without being choked up and stymied by the weeds. The root can develop in storms, rains, and sunshine.

The blessing is the recognition of this opportunity and the recognition of the growth. Opportunities are blessings. Gratitude for the opportunities leads to spiritual development. Every challenge is an opportunity. Recognition of the blessings provides the opportunity to develop your spirit. Challenges implore you to pray, and through prayer, trust will grow and the ego is weeded. This is the spiritual cycle for spiritual development.

THE PRESENT

Staying in the today moment is a challenge for most. We say plan; however, every moment cannot be planned for. Some moments need the time to reflect on what has transpired and how this moment was viewed, acted upon, impacted your life, or prepared you for a better tomorrow. Once that day has gone, it is in the past. It's harder to recall the words uttered once that day has passed.

You can start with asking: How did my day begin? Did I get up with ample time for prayer and meditation? Did I awaken with anger in my heart or love and peace in my spirit? In the beginning of the day, say words over the remainder of your day.

Introspection is how one changes the affected lives. You must become introspective if you seek to have a higher spirit. It is similar to a trade. You may learn how to sew using a pattern that starts out quite simple, but through practice and reflection, you will use a more complex pattern or become gifted to sew elegantly without a pattern. You develop an eye and hand that coordinate and create a masterpiece. For those who are carpenters, you may begin with making a simple box that grows into a bird feeder, which evolves into a storage bin with additional hinges, and then become a builder of homes following architectural plans.

This is the way of introspection and spiritual self-development. You begin with a prayer or meditation, and you only are seated for a short period in time and may become distracted, but through practice, you relax and let go. Each week or month you begin to breathe differently. Thoughts, writings, or messages enter your spirit, and they develop not to perfection but to abilities. Each one will hear his or her message and work on his or her own development—no rush, no measurement, no comparison because it is the work on the individual self.

The work is endless, and it comes in time. Who knows what the person next to you has endured and what path that person is on, so no one can judge or measure another's development. It is according to their previous incarnations, their connections to their ancestors, the work that they do in this incarnation, and their fortitude to do Our work.

Our work is your work. It is carving out your program, your steps, and your actions. Do not look over your shoulder to see, criticize, or discuss another's steps. Just map out your course, create your pattern, and build your spirit house. We don't look for glamour and frivolities. We look for a firm foundation that can hold up to the storms of life. Set your course, create your pattern, and build your spirit. This will bring you to a life everlasting. Our arms are open to those who persist, so stand tall after tripping and falling. Remain steadfast and persistent in the development of the spirit.

This is Our work for each one of you. Gather your tools of patience and persistence with the direction of introspection, and you will become satisfied with the outcome. This writing is to work on the present moment and develop your spirit over time. Start with this time and this moment—the present.

STILLNESS

Stillness is a state of being that few know about, and few desire an interest in stillness. Quieting oneself is the greatest step toward self-development. Quieting yourself to prayers and allowing thoughts to enter your spirit and receive messages is the greatest step in your progress. Watching and observing teachers gives you the ability to help, give suggestions, and coach others. If you are constantly chattering, you are unable to truly know the needs of others. The same is true of those attempting spiritual growth. The busyness impedes the progress toward insight (seeing within). Stillness requires work—but a different kind of work. It requires restraining the wings from flight and ceasing unnecessary conversations; it requires introspection and less outward thoughts. It involves thoughts about self and how progress can be made through stillness in life. It also allows us to implant the needed thoughts in order to grow and develop. Whose thoughts will you hear if you are constantly listening to the noises of your world? No barriers can prevail if stillness exists. No spiritual growth can develop without excellent listening skills.

How can you hear spiritual messages or have clear dreams when negative messages, noises, and emotions create the barriers that prevent spirit messages from being heard? Learn to sit with quiet time so that the correct words will flow when a conversation is needed; the correct steps are taken because you are going in the direction of your path.

Stillness is a state of being—being at one with the divine and being in a state of gratitude and clear understanding. It is a state of serenity. It heals all wounds because you are in a state of being and allowing us to have an impact on your being—more clearly, to have an impact on your spirit.

Meditations are meaningful and are not just for moments. Healing comes about through the stillness in life. It is the acquisition of patience in your spirit that heals you and makes you cognizant of the steps in your healing process whether it is physical, mental, or a spiritual healing. Many times it encompasses all factors. One may not recognize the need because of the constant conversations and the constant motion. It is more challenging to still yourself, but the rewards are greater.

Your plans are methodical, your steps are fewer but more directed, your emotions are controlled and understood, and your spirit rides the tranquil wave into an everlasting life of love and peace. You will be able to move more miles on a directed path than in a maze of undirected steps to an unknown path. Stillness is the greatest state of being.

When a person does not stop for moments before partaking in the next meal or give any thought to what they are eating, obesity can occur. This slows the process down so that one can realize that he or she needs to stop and think prior to eating a meal. Obesity can also be full with anger or full with a lack of direction. One lives an unfulfilling life, and so it is filled with physical food. A spiritual fullness will prevent obesity because food is not the substitute for fulfillment. You can never be hungry when you are spiritually fed. We are not saying to never eat because you are in human form, but your primary nourishment is for your spirit to receive its nurturing. That will lead the body to receive what it needs.

Healing comes through spirit senses—what to do and how to do it, how often, and more. These are just examples of how stillness can affect lives. Answers are not received unless one has a bended ear. Bended ears are on those who know it is time to still themselves and listen. Stillness is a state of being that prepares and clears the path for a highly elevated spiritual life.

Scribes practice the art of stillness; otherwise, Our messages are not transmitted. Stillness is a prescription for all. You will reap many benefits from the harvest when seeds are sown with stillness.

ABOUT THE SCRIBE

Karen Njeri King was born in New York City and raised in Brooklyn, New York. She spent many years working in the educational field serving children, parents, teachers, and administrators. Whether volunteering at free breakfast programs, leading after-school programs, or conducting workshops, Njeri always finds time to give back to her community. While working with teens, she became one of the founding members of the Sojourner Truth Adolescent Rites Society (STARS) and coauthored the book *Transformation: A Rites of Passage Manual for African American Girls.*

After receiving training in the Akan tradition, Njeri, the scribe, spent time in Ghana, West Africa, visiting with an elderly Densu priestess by the name of Nana Okorewah. Her grandmother was, in fact, a priestess to the Akan deity: Maame Senyani. Maame Senyani is the spirit that she is channeling in the writings included in this book. She uses the term *scribe* to be clear that the messages received were put in written form, which led to the creation of the book.

Njeri spends time with her mother, daughters, sons, and grandchildren while constantly seeking knowledge and working toward keeping herself on a spiritual journey.